At Sylvan, we believe reading is one of life's most important and enriching abilities, and we're glad you've chosen our resources to help your child build these critically important skills. We know that the time you spend with your child reinforcing the lessons learned in school will contribute to his love of reading. This love of reading will translate into academic achievement. A successful reader is ready for the world around him, ready to do research, ready to experience the world of literature, and prepared to make the connections necessary to achieve in school and in life.

We use a research-based, step-by-step process in teaching reading at Sylvan that includes thought-provoking reading selections and activities. As students increase their success as readers they become more confident. With increasing confidence, students build even more success. Our Sylvan workbooks are designed to help you to help your child build the skills and confidence that will contribute to your child's success in school.

We're excited to partner with you to support the development of confident, well-prepared independent learners!

The Sylvan Team

Sylvan Learning Center.
Unleash your child's potential here.

No matter how big or small the academic challenge, every child has the ability to learn. But sometimes children need help making it happen. Sylvan believes every child has the potential to do great things. And we know better than anyone else how to tap into that academic potential so that a child's future really is full of possibilities. Sylvan Learning Center is the place where your child can build and master the learning skills needed to succeed and unlock the potential you know is there.

The proven, personalized approach of our in-center programs deliver unparalleled results that other supplemental education services simply can't match. Your child's achievements will be seen not only in test scores and report cards but outside the classroom as well. And when he starts achieving his full potential, everyone will know it. You will see a new level of confidence come through in everything he does and every interaction he has.

How can Sylvan's personalized in-center approach help your child unleash his potential?

- Starting with our exclusive Sylvan Skills Assessment®, we pinpoint your child's exact academic needs.

- Then we develop a customized learning plan designed to achieve your child's academic goals.

- Through our method of skill mastery, your child will not only learn and master every skill in his personalized plan, he will be truly motivated and inspired to achieve his full potential.

To get started, simply contact your local Sylvan Learning Center to set up an appointment. And to learn more about Sylvan and our innovative in-center programs, call 1-800-EDUCATE or visit www.SylvanLearning.com. *With over 850 locations in North America, there is a Sylvan Learning Center near you!*

2nd Grade
Jumbo Language Arts Success
Workbook

Published in the United States by Random House, Inc., New York, and in Canada by Random House of Canada Limited, Toronto.

This book was previously published with the title *2nd Grade Language Arts Success* as a trade paperback by Sylvan Learning, Inc., an imprint of Penguin Random House LLC, in 2009.

www.sylvanlearning.com

Created by Smarterville Productions LLC
Producer: TJ Trochlil McGreevy
Producer & Editorial Direction: The Linguistic Edge
Writers: Christina Wilsdon (Reading Skill Builders), Michael Artin (Spelling Games & Activities),
Margaret Crocker (Vocabulary Puzzles)
Cover and Interior Illustrations: Duendes del Sur, Delfin Barral, and Shawn Finley
Layout and Art Direction: SunDried Penguin
Art Manager: Adina Ficano

First Edition

ISBN: 978-0-375-43031-2

Library of Congress Cataloging-in-Publication Data available upon request.

This book is available at special discounts for bulk purchases for sales promotions or premiums.
For more information, write to Special Markets/Premium Sales, 1745 Broadway, MD 6-2,
New York, New York 10019 or e-mail specialmarkets@randomhouse.com.

PRINTED IN CHINA

12

Reading Skill Builders Contents

Spelling Games & Activities Contents

Vocabulary Puzzles Contents

2nd Grade
Reading Skill Builders

Blend Two Consonants

Sort It Out

What do you call a blend of two consonants? A **consonant blend**, of course! Each letter makes its own sound but also blends with its buddy's sound, as in words like *fly*, *plate*, and *train*.

SORT the words. PUT the words into the lists. WRITE them on the blanks.

flip   break   cloud   black   grape   clam   blue   green
clock   block   bring   flower   brave   ground   floppy

br
break
bring
brave

cl
clock
clam
cloud

fl
flower
flip
floppy

gr
green
ground
grape

bl
block
blue
black

Herd That Word

Yee haw! Cowgirl Kris has to round up words with the right consonant blends. Help her find them!

LOOK at the blend next to each fence. READ the words inside the fence. CIRCLE the word that starts with the correct blend.

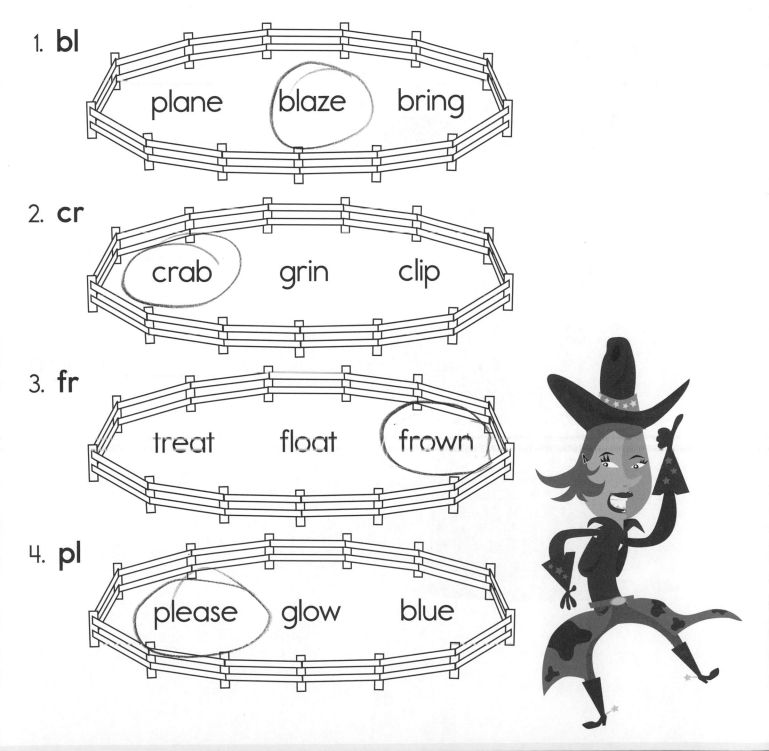

1. **bl**

plane · blaze · bring

2. **cr**

crab · grin · clip

3. **fr**

treat · float · frown

4. **pl**

please · glow · blue

Blend Two Consonants

Blender Blunder

Uh-oh! Somebody spilled words into the blender. They got chopped up. Can you put them back together?

LOOK at the consonant blends in the blender. MATCH each blend with the right ending. FILL IN the blanks with the correct blends.

br   dr

fl   tr

cl

bl

1. _____ ouse

2. _____ oud

3. _____ ave

4. _____ ive

5. _____ oor

6. _____ iangle

You've Got Mail

The letter "s" is friends with many consonants. It's in the blends missing from this e-mail.

LOOK at the consonant blends word box. FILL IN the blanks with the right blends. You can use blends more than once.

| sc | sk | sl | sm | sn | sp | st | sw |

Wow! Today I flew down a _____eep hill on my

_____ateboard. I went so fast, the wheels made _____oke.

It was _____eet! But I had to _____ow down and _____in

sideways when a _____unk suddenly crawled across the

street like a tired _____ail, or else it would have made a big

_____ink. _____ary!

Blend Two Consonants

Who Says?

Yakkity-yak! Who's saying that?

READ each sentence. CIRCLE the beginning blends that repeat three times in each sentence. MATCH sentences with names. DRAW lines between them.

HINT: Each speaker uses three words with blends that match the blend in his or her name.

1. I'm (cr)abby because a (cr)ocodile ate my (cr)ayon.

Trixie

2. There's a spot of spinach on my spoon.

Francis

3. I ate a snack and made a snake snowman.

Craig

4. My frog likes French fries.

Snowden

5. A troll on a tractor is trouble.

Placido

6. Please don't put your plant on my plate.

Spencer

Sound Search

OK, detective. Track down consonant blends in this story.

READ the story. CIRCLE each word that starts with a consonant blend. FILL IN the blanks with the words.

The people of France couldn't sleep because a creepy dragon prowled the land. It crushed houses every night. Its claws broke branches off trees. Its breath fried the grass. What a problem!

One night, it tried to trap the prince. But then it yelped and flew away. "It's scared of me," said a grinning spider sitting on the ground nearby. "Pretty great!"

You've Got Mail

Some blends are made up of three consonant sounds. The letter "s" pops up a lot, as in *spread*, *square*, and *stroke*.

LOOK at the consonant blends in the word box. FILL IN the blanks in the e-mail with the right blends. You can use blends more than once.

scr	spl	squ	str

A really _____ange thing happened today. I was eating a

bowl of _____awberry ice cream when I heard a loud

_____eech. Then I heard a _____eak and a _____awk.

I jumped up to look out the window and saw a noisy

_____uggle going on between a _____irrel and a bird. They

were playing tug-of-war with a _____ing! Suddenly the bird

let go. The _____uirrel fell into the _____eam with a _____ash.

I sat down in surprise. Whoops. I _____ashed

my ice cream—and let out a _____eam!

Sort It Out

SORT the words. PUT the words into the lists.

square	stripe	squash	screech	spray	split	scram	strike
spread	street	splat	spring	squirm	scream	splash	

spr

_____

_____

_____

squ

_____

_____

_____

spl

_____

_____

_____

scr

_____

_____

_____

str

_____

_____

_____

End with a Blend

Herd That Word

Words sometimes end with consonant blends, as in *elf*, *pump*, and *bent*. Cowgirl Pearl is busy rounding up some correct blends at the end of words!

LOOK at the blend next to each fence. READ the words inside the fence. CIRCLE the word that ends with the correct blend.

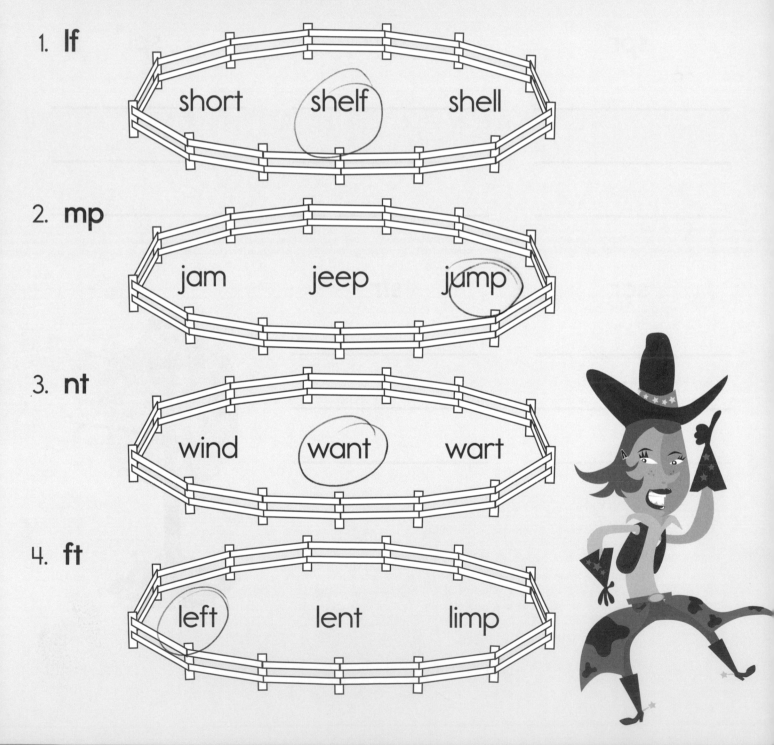

1. **lf**

   short   (shelf)   shell

2. **mp**

   jam   jeep   (jump)

3. **nt**

   wind   (want)   wart

4. **ft**

   (left)   lent   limp

Who Says?

READ each sentence. CIRCLE the final blends that repeat three times in each sentence. MATCH sentences with names. DRAW lines between them.

HINT: Each sentence has three words that end with the same blend. Each name ends in a blend too.

1. The wind blew my towel and hat off the sand.   Hank

2. Honk if you'd like a pink tank!   Millicent

3. I did not need a potato, but my aunt went and sent me one.   Fisk

4. I saw her jump off the ramp into the swamp.   Desmond

5. The best horses in the West run fast.   Amethyst

6. Ask the elephant to do the task with its tusk.   Kemp

Blender Blunder

LOOK at the final blends in the blender. MATCH each blend with the right beginning. FILL IN the blanks with the correct blends.

ft

nt

mp

lt

st

nk

1. breakfa _st_____

2. so_____

3. se_____

4. fe_____

5. su_____

6. swa_____

What's This?

LOOK at each picture. READ the words next to it. CIRCLE the correct word.

HINT: Keep an eye on those end blends!

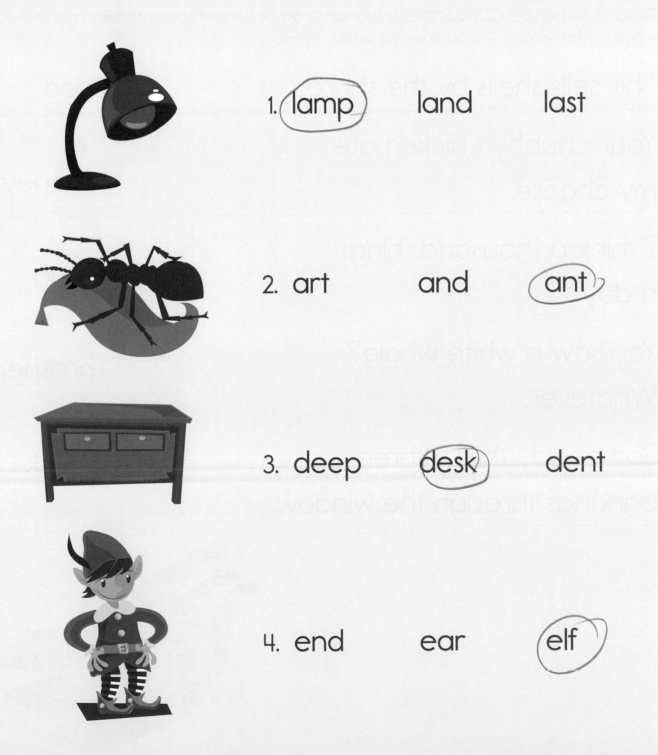

1. (lamp)   land   last

2. art   and   (ant)

3. deep   (desk)   dent

4. end   ear   (elf)

Consonant Combos

Who Says?

Some consonant letters pair up to make a whole new sound, as in *cheer*, *fish*, and *thump*. We call these teams **consonant combos**. Check these chats for consonant combos. Each name shares a combo with one sentence.

READ each sentence. CIRCLE the consonant combos that repeat three times. MATCH sentences with names. DRAW lines between them.

1. She sells shells by the shore.

2. Your chubby chicken ate my cheese.

3. I think a thousand things a day.

4. You saw a white whale? Whatever.

5. Somebody threw three bananas through the window.

Theo

Whitney

Sheila

Thrasher

Chuck

Blender Blunder

LOOK at the consonant combos in the blender. MATCH each consonant combo with the right ending. FILL IN the blanks with the correct consonant combos.

1. _____eese

2. _____eel

3. _____under

4. _____ead

5. _____ark

Consonant Combos

Herd That Word

The consonant combo "ng" sounds like the "ing" in *bring* when it's at the end of a word. The consonant combo "gh" often sounds like **f** at a word's end. Help Cowgirl Spring look for words that end in these consonant combos.

LOOK at the consonant combo next to each fence. READ the words inside the fence. CIRCLE the word that ends with the correct combo.

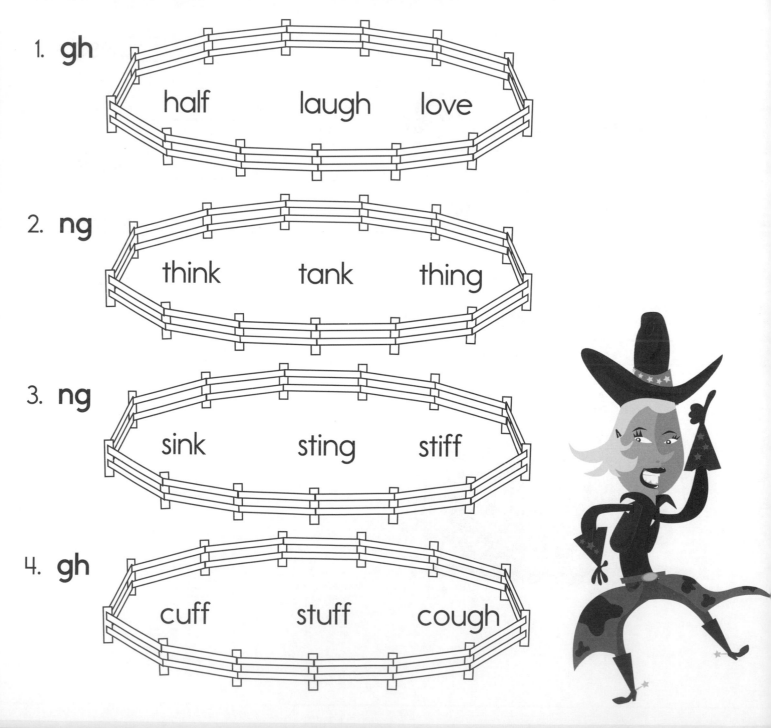

1. **gh**

half　　　laugh　　　love

2. **ng**

think　　　tank　　　thing

3. **ng**

sink　　　sting　　　stiff

4. **gh**

cuff　　　stuff　　　cough

Say Hey!

READ the sentences. FILL IN the blanks with words from the word box.

HINT: Each missing word contains a consonant combo and rhymes with a word next to it in the sentence.

laugh	sting	tough	rang	song	rough

1. A piece of sandpaper is _____ stuff!

2. Does that buzzing thing _____?

3. That's only a little funny, so I'll just half _____.

4. The singer sang a very, very long _____.

5. Then he took out bells and _____, sang, and danced!

6. That rope will break because it's not _____ enough.

Hard or Soft?

Sound Search

The letter "c" can sound like either **k** or **s**. Hard "c" sounds like **k**, as in *cold*. Soft "c" sounds like **s**, as in *cent*. "C" if you can find them in this story!

READ the story. CIRCLE words that start with hard "c." DRAW a line under words that start with soft "c." FILL IN the blanks with the words.

Sassy the dog followed the tracks of Cinnamon the cat into a cave. A cold wind blew. Cobwebs hung from the ceiling. Centipedes ran across the floor. Suddenly she heard "meow" . . . and "tweet"! There in the center of a circle of rocks was the kitty—with a stolen canary!

Hard c	Soft c
_____	_____
_____	_____
_____	_____
_____	_____
_____	_____

Follow That Sound

START at the arrow. DRAW a line along the path that is lined with words that start with a hard "c" to get to the cupcake.

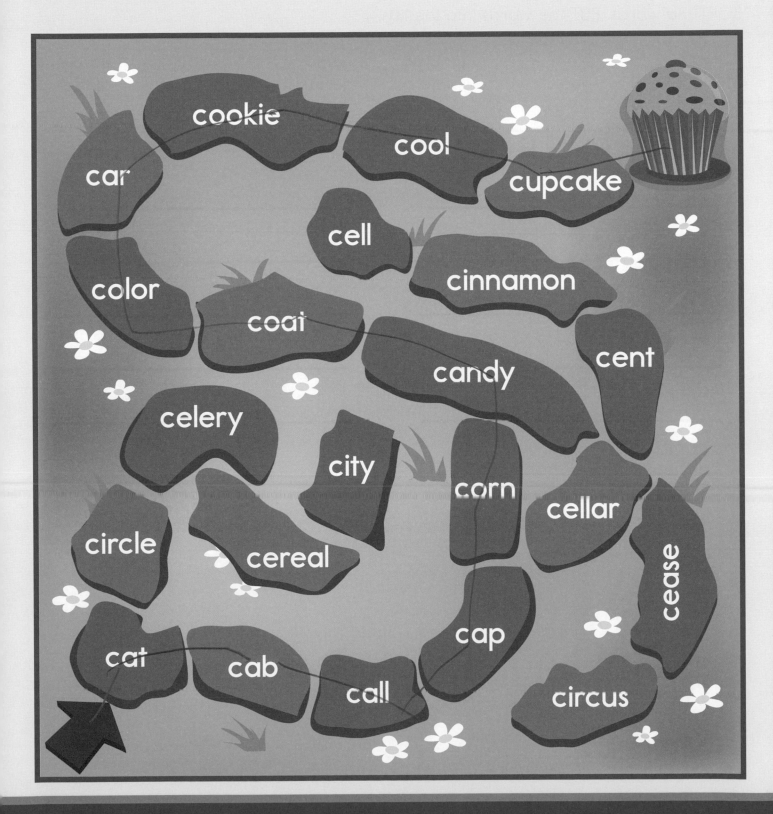

cookie

cool

cupcake

car

cell

color

cinnamon

coat

cent

candy

celery

city

corn

cellar

circle

cereal

cease

cat

cab

call

cap

circus

19

Hard or Soft?

Sort It Out

The letter "g" can be hard or soft too. A hard "g" sounds like the **g** in *goose*. A soft "g" sounds like **j**, as in *gem*.

SORT the words. PUT the words into the lists.

| gab | giant | general | game | giraffe | garden |
| gobble | goat | gentle | germ | girl | ginger |

Hard **g**

_____

_____

_____

_____

_____

_____

Soft **g**

_____

_____

_____

_____

_____

_____

Herd That Word

Giddy-up! Cowgirl Gina has a hard job, but she's no softie. Gee-haw!

LOOK at the "g" next to each fence. READ the words inside the fence. CIRCLE the word that starts with the correct sound.

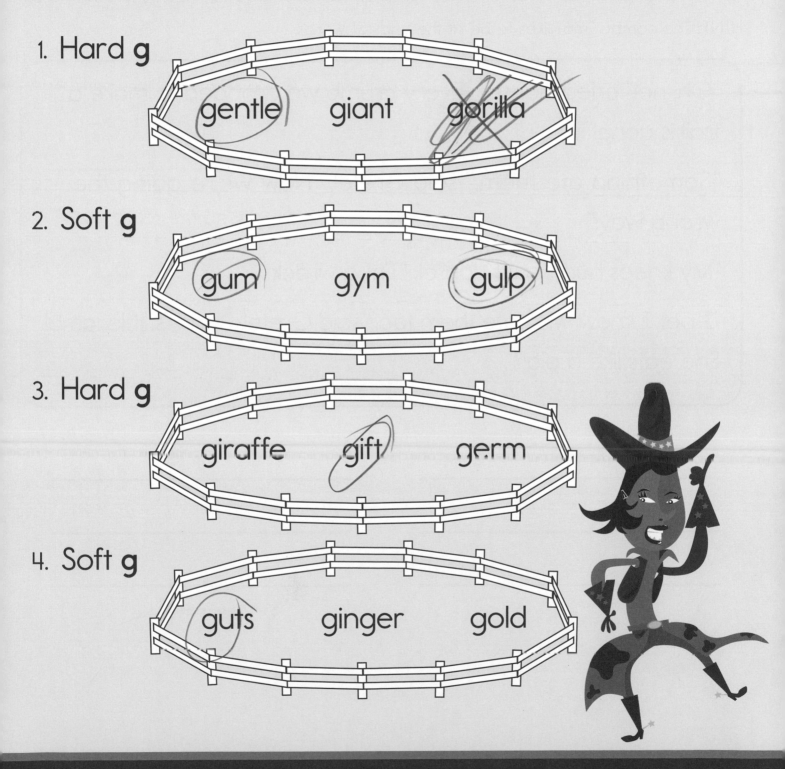

1. Hard **g**

gentle   giant   gorilla

2. Soft **g**

gum   gym   gulp

3. Hard **g**

giraffe   gift   germ

4. Soft **g**

guts   ginger   gold

Sound Search

You can see them, but you can't hear them! They're letters in the **silent** consonant combos "kn," "wr," and "mb." The "k," "w," and "b" don't make a peep. See if you can find words with silent consonant combos in this story.

READ the story. CIRCLE words with silent consonant combos. FILL IN the blanks with the words.

HINT: The combo "mb" likes to be at the ends of words.

"Oh, no!" cried Hansel. "Every crumb we dropped to make a trail is gone!"

"Something ate them," said Gretel. "Now we're going the wrong way!"

"My knees hurt," said Hansel. "I'm a wreck!"

"I bet I know who ate them too," said Gretel. "Mary's little lamb! She eats like a pig!"

_____   _____

_____   _____

_____   _____

What's This?

LOOK at each picture. READ the words next to it. CIRCLE the correct word.

HINT: *Shh*! The correct word has a silent consonant combo in it!

1. night   knight   knot

2. come   cob   comb

3. writer   water   wrong

4. nee   knee   kneel

Final "E"–Finally!

Build It

The letter "e" is powerful when it's at the end of a word. It can change the word's sound by making its vowel long! *Hat*, for example, turns into *hate*.

ADD a final "e" to each word. FILL IN the blanks with the new words.

1. cut + e = _____

2. dim + e = _____

3. fin + e = _____

4. fir + e = _____

5. kit + e = _____

6. mad + e = _____

7. pin + e = _____

8. plan + e = _____

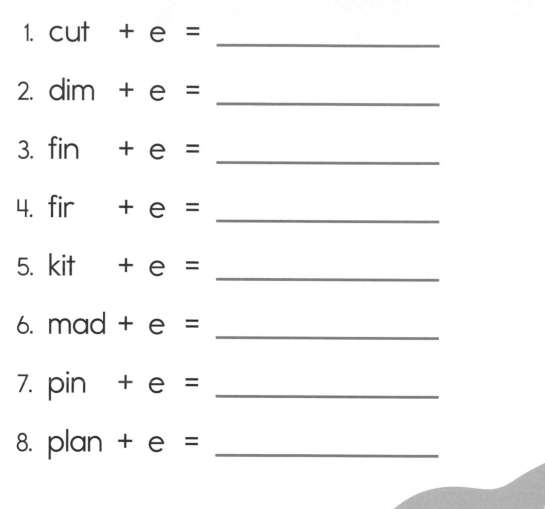

Sound Search

READ the story. CIRCLE the words that have a final "e" that makes another vowel long.
FILL IN the blanks with the words.

A mole stuck its nose out of the ground.

"Looks fine, Elly," he said.

Elly came out too. "I hate the sun," she said, blinking.

So they crawled to the shade of a pine by the lake. Suddenly a scary shape flew over—but it was just a plane. Then another scary thing appeared—but it was just a kite.

But the third time, Zak shouted, "Hide! Dive into the hole!"

"How rude," said the mule. "I just wanted to tell them a joke."

_____   _____   _____

_____   _____   _____

_____   _____   _____

_____   _____   _____

_____   _____   _____

Get a Long, Li'l Vowel

Yo, Poet!

The letter "a" in *same* is a long vowel. But vowels can team up to sound like **a** too. These teams include "ei," "ai," and "ay."

READ the poem. FILL IN the blanks with long **a** words from the word box.

pain	play	wail	way	eight
gray	jail	pails	rain	

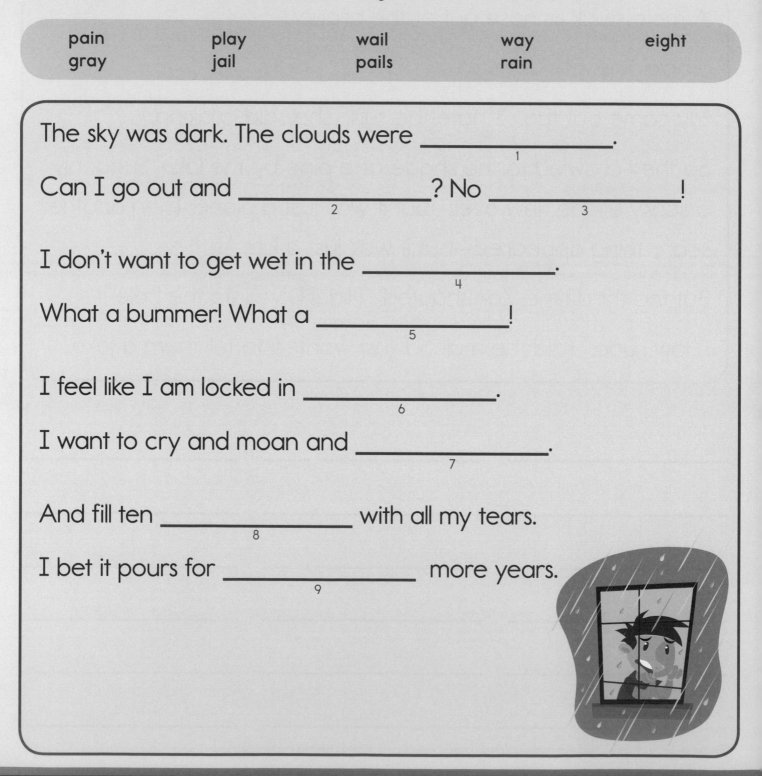

The sky was dark. The clouds were _____.
1

Can I go out and _____? No _____!
2   3

I don't want to get wet in the _____.
4

What a bummer! What a _____!
5

I feel like I am locked in _____.
6

I want to cry and moan and _____.
7

And fill ten _____ with all my tears.
8

I bet it pours for _____ more years.
9

Follow That Sound

START at the arrow. DRAW a line along the path filled with words that have a long **a** sound to get to the amazing brain.

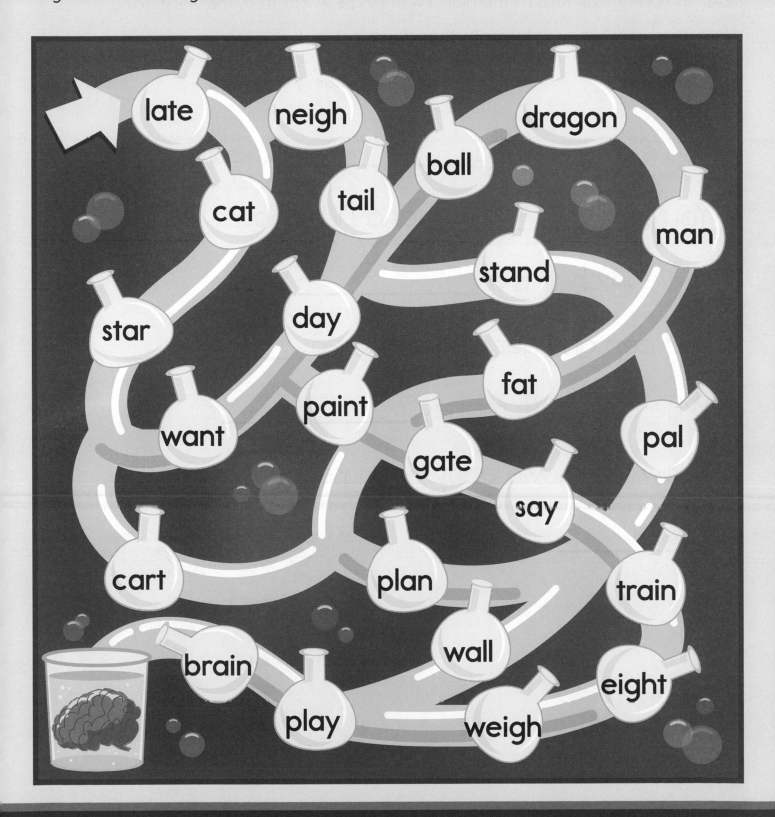

Get a Long, Li'l Vowel

Say Hey!

See an "e," "ea," "ee," or "ey," and you may hear long **e**!

READ the sentences. FILL IN the blanks with long **e** words from the word box.

HINT: The correct word rhymes with a word next to it.

sheep	sneak	neat	honey	seal	me

1. Fish is a very good _____ meal.

2. You be _____ and I'll be you!

3. A clean chair is a _____ seat.

4. Bo Peep and her sisters all keep _____.

5. Where is all the money, _____?

6. I saw the movie early because I got a

   _____ peek.

Herd That Word

Yee-haw! Long **e** can't flee when it's seen by Cowgirl Jean.

LOOK at the spelling of the long **e** sound next to each fence. READ the words inside the fence. CIRCLE the word that has the correct spelling of long **e**.

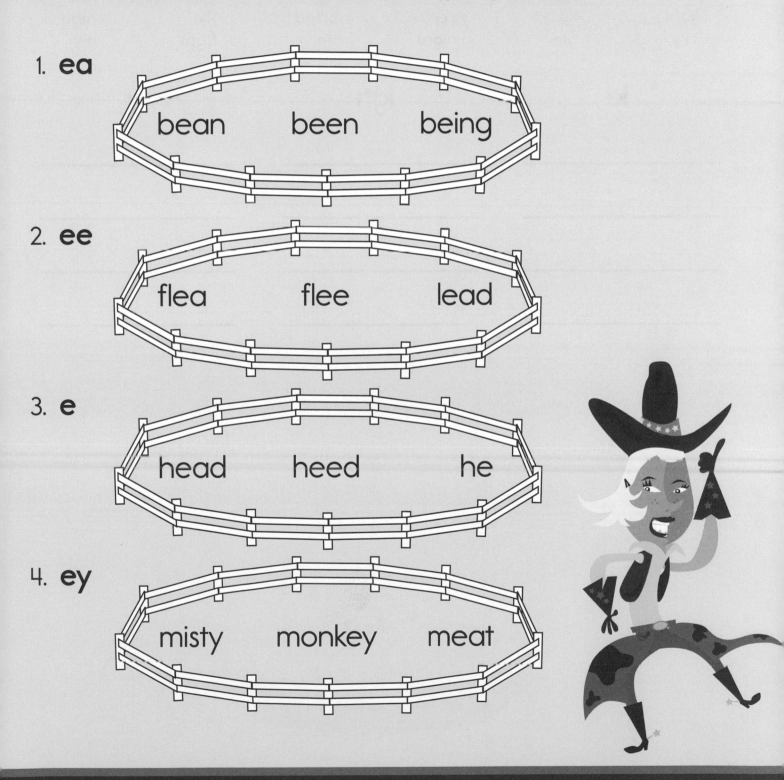

1. **ea**

bean   been   being

2. **ee**

flea   flee   lead

3. **e**

head   heed   he

4. **ey**

misty   monkey   meat

Sort It Out

Long **i** can be spelled "ie," "igh," and "y." Listen for it in *die*, *tight*, and *July*.

SORT the words. PUT the words into the lists.

| light | lie | sky | cried | fly | high |
| cry | pie | night | tie | fight | my |

ie	**igh**	**y**
_____	_____	_____
_____	_____	_____
_____	_____	_____
_____	_____	_____

Sound Search

"I spy with my little eye a word with long i!"

READ the story. CIRCLE words with the long i sound. FILL IN the blanks with the words.

Chef Toasty cooked all night long to bake the perfect pie. Just as the sky grew light, he put it on a high shelf. "My delight," he sighed. Chef shooed away a fly. Then he lay down for a nap. But a sly fox sneaked in a window. He grabbed the treat and ran. "Alas," cried Chef.

Would he bake a new one? He could try.

_____   _____   _____

_____   _____   _____

_____   _____   _____

_____   _____   _____

Get a Long, Li'l Vowel

Herd That Word

Oh, give me a home…. Cowgirl Roma goes where long **o** roams! It can be spelled "o," "oa," or "ow."

LOOK at the spelling of the long **o** sound next to each fence. READ the words inside the fence. CIRCLE the word that has the correct spelling of long **o**.

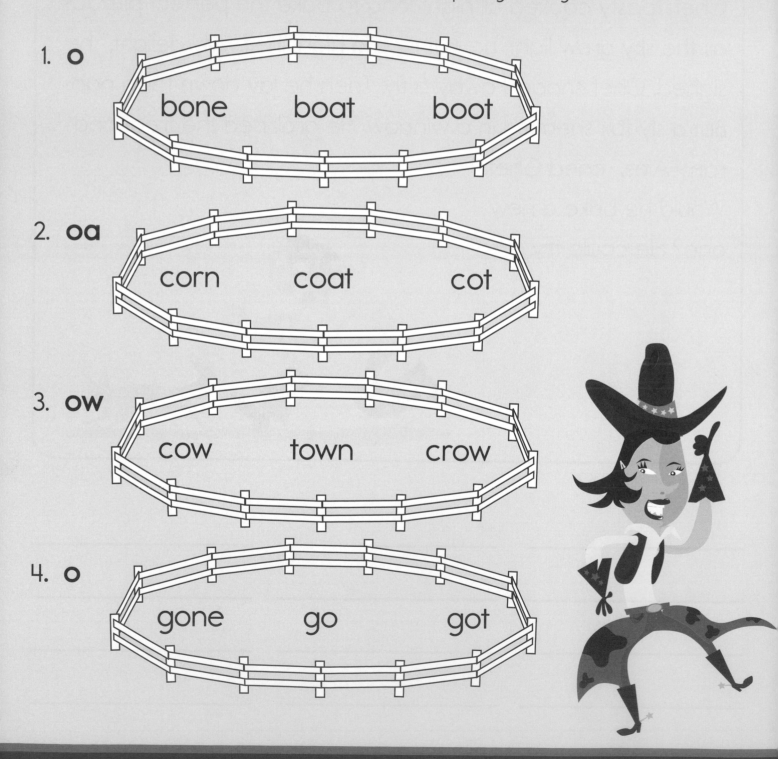

1. **o**

bone   boat   boot

2. **oa**

corn   coat   cot

3. **ow**

cow   town   crow

4. **o**

gone   go   got

Yo, Poet!

READ the poem. FILL IN the blanks with long **o** words from the word box.

gold	holes	toast	slow	cold
potatoes	boat	soap	cocoa	

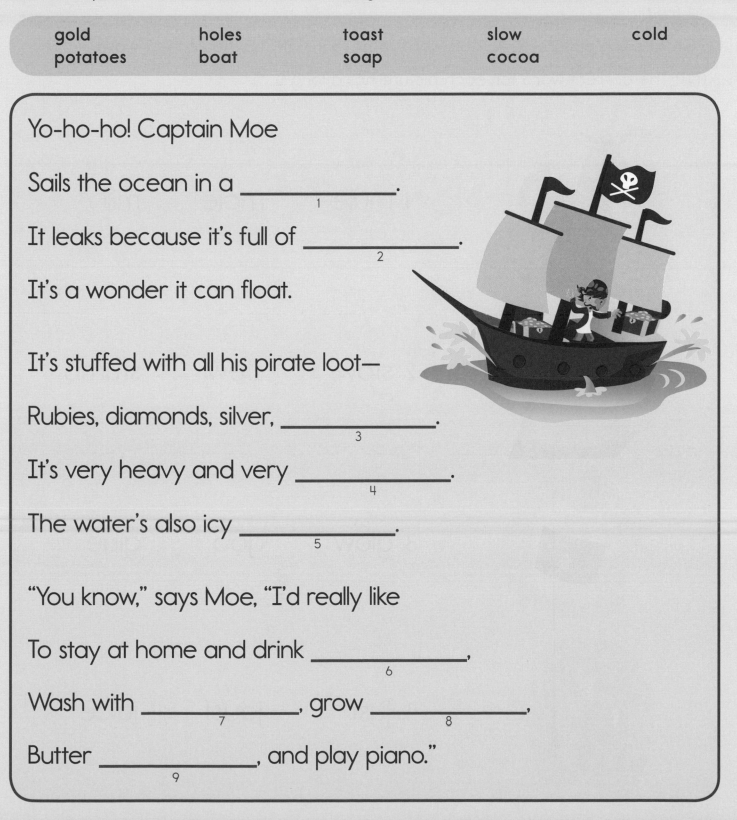

Yo-ho-ho! Captain Moe

Sails the ocean in a _____.
                        1

It leaks because it's full of _____.
                                2

It's a wonder it can float.

It's stuffed with all his pirate loot—

Rubies, diamonds, silver, _____.
                              3

It's very heavy and very _____.
                            4

The water's also icy _____.
                        5

"You know," says Moe, "I'd really like

To stay at home and drink _____,
                             6

Wash with _____, grow _____,
             7   8

Butter _____, and play piano."
          9

Get a Long, Li'l Vowel

What's This?

Hey, you! Long **u** can be spelled "u," "ew," "ue," and "ui." Examples are *music, chew, fuel,* and *fruit.*

LOOK at each picture. READ the words next to it. CIRCLE the correct word.

HINT: The correct word for each picture has a long **u**.

1. mule   mole   mill

2. stow   stew   stump

3. glow   goo   glue

4. just   joust   juice

Say Hey!

READ the sentences. FILL IN the blanks with long **u** words from the list.

HINT: The correct word rhymes with a word next to it.

unicorn	knew	new	blue	juice	flu

1. There are some red, some green, and a few

   _____.

2. The _____, you know, is worse than a really

   bad cold.

3. Some people think a _____ horn is magic.

4. Would you like some _____, Bruce?

5. The crew _____ it was time to take off.

6. I think I have discovered a

   _____ clue!

Because "R" Says So!

Sort It Out

The letter "r" is the boss of vowels. It changes their sounds. Check out bossy "r" at work in "er," "ir," and "ur," as in *her*, *fir*, and *blur*.

SORT the words. PUT the words into the lists. WRITE them on the blanks.

first	burp	dinner	fur	dirt	curl
herd	bird	paper	turn	germ	girl

er	**ir**	**ur**
_____	_____	_____
_____	_____	_____
_____	_____	_____
_____	_____	_____

Sound Search

Okay, detective. See if you can find the words with "er," "ir," and "ur" in them.
READ the story. CIRCLE words with the r sound. FILL IN the blanks with the words.

Bill the Bird invited Shelly the Turtle to dinner. He set the table with his best purple dishes and silver. Then he waited. And waited.

"Bad manners!" he thought when Shelly finally walked in—slowly. He stirred the soup.

"Ew, germs," thought Shelly, looking at her dirty dish. Suddenly a loud burp shook the table.

"Surprise!" said a voice. A spider popped up. "I ate first because it's my birthday."

_____   _____   _____

_____   _____   _____

_____   _____   _____

_____   _____   _____

Because "R" Says So!

What's This?

The letter "r" can make vowels say **or** even if they're spelled with an "ar," "or," "ore," or "our." Some examples are *wart*, *porch*, *more*, and *pour*.

LOOK AT each picture. READ the words next to it. CIRCLE the correct word.

1. weird   award   word

2. horse   hours   house

3. cork   chore   core

4. for   fur   four

Say Hey!

These sentences need words with bossy "r" in them.

READ the sentences. FILL IN the blanks with words from the list.

HINT: The correct word rhymes with a word next to it.

award	fork	wart	torn	bored	pour

1. I eat ham with a pork _____.

2. The jester did not make the _____ lord laugh.

3. Everyone loves her, so she won the Most Adored _____.

4. Please _____ four glasses of milk.

5. My old shirt is worn, _____, and dirty.

6. I named my dragon Snort-_____.

Because "R" Says So!

Herd That Word

The letter "r" makes "air," "are," and "ear" sound like **air** in many words, as in *fair*, *care*, and *tear*. Help Cowgirl Clair rope 'em!

LOOK at the spelling next to each fence. READ the words inside the fence. CIRCLE the word that has the correct spelling.

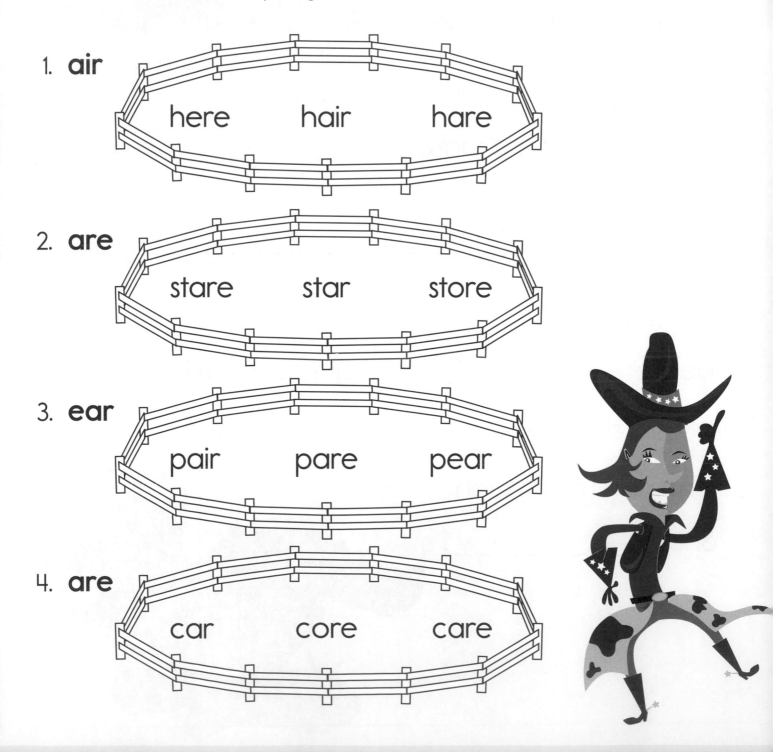

1. **air**

here   hair   hare

2. **are**

stare   star   store

3. **ear**

pair   pare   pear

4. **are**

car   core   care

Yo, Poet!

READ the poem. FILL IN the blanks with long **a** words from the list.

bear	stare	pair	care
hair	bare	fair	underwear

Fuzzy-wuzzy was a _____.
1

Fuzzy-wuzzy had no _____.
2

Other bears would stop and _____.
3

Fuzzy, he just didn't _____.
4

He had mittens—a nice red _____—
5

And toasty winter _____.
6

But still it isn't really _____
7

For a bear to be all _____.
8

Going for a Glide

Say Hey!

Sometimes letters just glide together to make a new vowel sound. The pairs "oi" and "oy," for example, make the sound **oy** as in *join* and *joy*.

READ the sentences. FILL IN the blanks with words from the word box.

HINT: The correct word rhymes with a word next to it.

oyster	oil	boy	soil	toys	noise

1. Watch out for that kid—she destroys _____!

2. Be very careful when you boil _____.

3. A very wet shellfish is a moister _____.

4. Knock off all that _____, boys!

5. The queen's flowers grow in royal _____.

6. Is your cat a girl or a _____, Troy?

What's This?

Oy! Each picture here needs a label with the letters that glide together.

LOOK AT each picture. READ the words next to it. CIRCLE the correct word.

1. buy   boy   boil

2. nose   knees   noise

3. eel   oil   ail

4. toy   toil   toe

Herd That Word

Yow! Cowgirl Wow is out to pounce on "ou" and "ow"! Both spellings can sound like **ow**.

LOOK at the spelling of the **ow** sound next to each fence. READ the words inside the fence. CIRCLE the word that has the correct spelling.

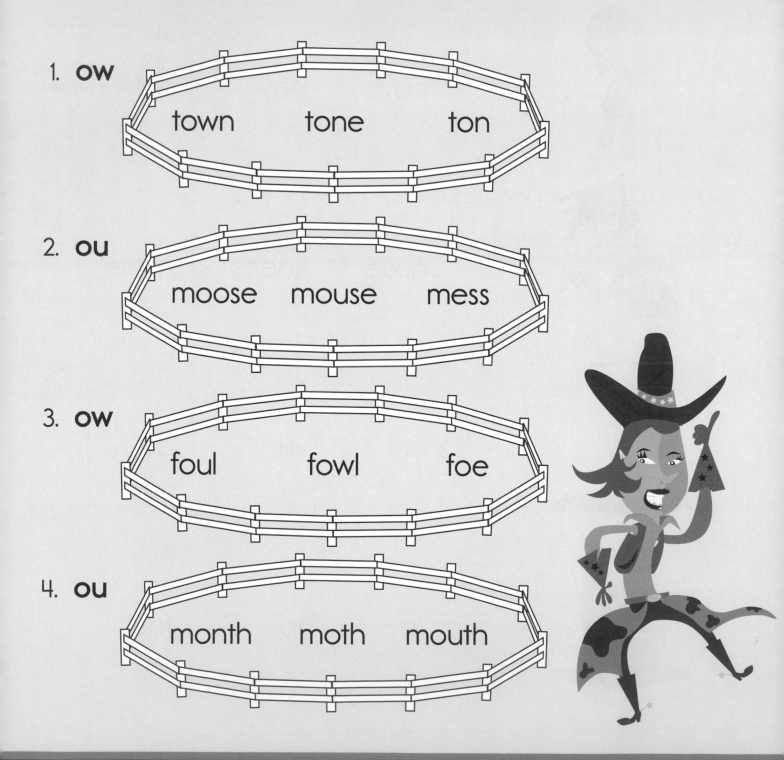

1. **ow**

town   tone   ton

2. **ou**

moose   mouse   mess

3. **ow**

foul   fowl   foe

4. **ou**

month   moth   mouth

Sound Search

READ the story. CIRCLE words that contain "ou" or "ow." FILL IN the blanks with the words.

"Wow!" said the brown hound dog as he looked at the fish in the fountain. "Look what I found. Trout!" His mouth watered. He crouched. Then he pounced. Splash!

"Help!" howled the dog. "I'm going to drown!"

Bess the Cow heard the loud sounds. So did Zeke the mouse. Together, they pulled the dog out.

"Stick to dog chow from now on," said Zeke.

_____   _____

_____   _____

_____   _____

_____   _____

_____   _____

_____   _____

Oo, Goo, Good

Sort It Out

You go "moo" like a cow when you say the **oo** sound in *moon*. But "oo" can also sound like the **oo** in *book*. We'll call them the "Goo **oo**" and the "Good **oo**."

SORT the words. PUT the words into the lists.

| hook | boot | food | look | poodle | cook |
| tooth | cool | wood | foot | school | took |

Goo oo

_____

_____

_____

_____

_____

Good oo

_____

_____

_____

_____

_____

Yo, Poet!

READ the poem. FILL IN the blanks with **oo** words from the word box.

| food | good | Shoo | zoo | moose |
| room | drool | books | zoom | goose |

There is a creature in my _____.

1

It likes to run and zip and _____.

2

It has feathers like a _____

3

And antlers like a big brown _____.

4

You might think that this is cool.

But you should see it drip and _____!

5

It gives me nasty, evil looks,

Eats my _____ and library _____.

6   7

It doesn't smell _____. It belongs in a _____.

8   9

But it won't go when I tell it, "_____!"

10

What's This?

You can hear an **aw** sound in words spelled with "aw." But the "a" in "al" and "all" sometimes says **aw** too! Examples are *straw*, *walk*, and *wall*.

LOOK at each picture. READ the words next to it. CIRCLE the correct word.

1. bawl   ball   bale

2. yawn   yarn   yen

3. hank   hunk   hawk

4. chick   check   chalk

Say Hey!

Awww, each sentence is missing a word!

READ the sentences. FILL IN the blanks with words from the word box.

HINT: The correct word rhymes with a word next to it.

| small | wall | claws | talk | bawl | dawn |

1. All my baby sister does is crawl, _____, and sleep.

2. At _____, Fawn wakes up because she's an early riser.

3. Humpty-Dumpty had a bad fall off the tall _____.

4. You use a very _____ ball to play Ping-Pong.

5. I can walk, _____, and chew gum at the same time.

6. Who painted my cat's paws _____ red?

Compound Words

Build It

A **compound word** is a word that's made up of two words put together, like *notebook* and *toadstool*.

ADD each pair of words. FILL IN the blanks with the new compound words.

1. bull + dog = _bulldog_

2. snow + man = _snowman_

3. black + berry = _____

4. cup + cake = _____

5. ginger + bread = _____

6. news + paper = _____

7. pop + corn = _____

8. bath + room = _____

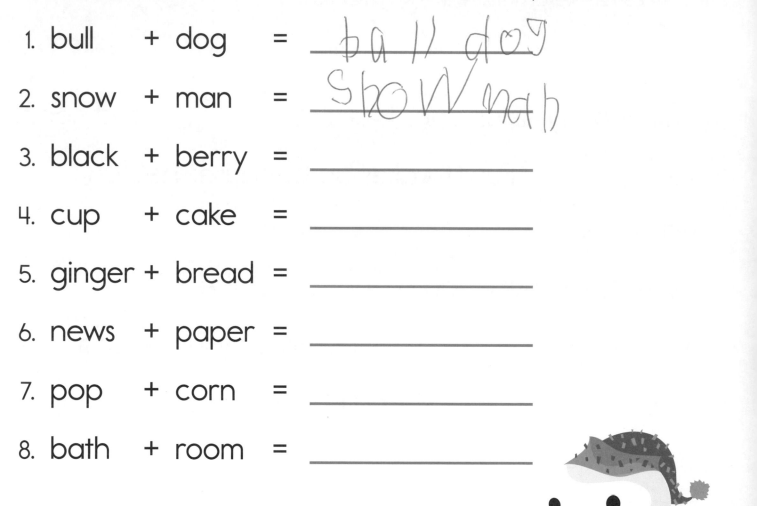

Break It Up

Split a compound word, and you get two words. *Firefighter*, for example, gives you *fire* and *fighter*. What a deal!

SPLIT each compound word. FILL IN the blanks with the two words.

1. daylight   = _____ + _____

2. railroad   = _____ + _____

3. toothbrush = _____ + _____

4. skateboard = _____ + _____

5. pinecone   = _____ + _____

6. baseball   = _____ + _____

7. suitcase   = _____ + _____

8. starfish   = _____ + _____

Compound Words

Match the Socks

READ the words on the socks. MATCH each sock with another sock to form a compund word. COLOR the socks so they match.

Blender Blunder

LOOK at the words in the blender. MATCH each word with a word in the list.
FILL IN the blanks with the correct words.

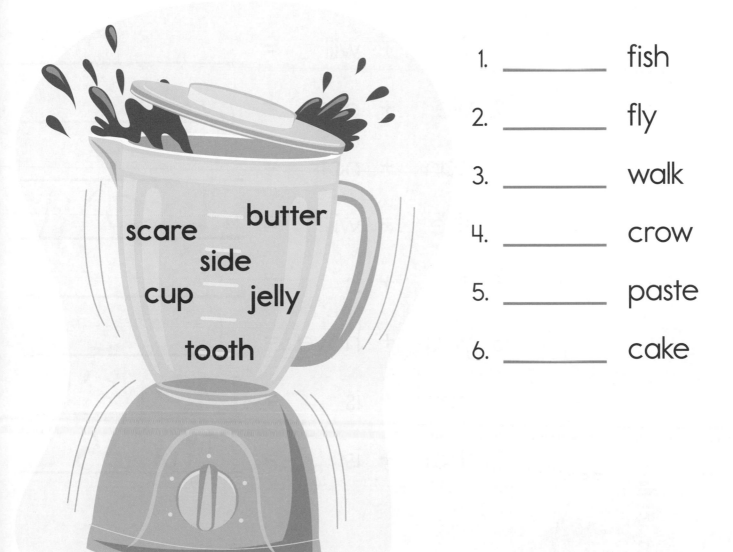

scare butter side cup jelly tooth

1. _____ fish

2. _____ fly

3. _____ walk

4. _____ crow

5. _____ paste

6. _____ cake

Build It

Speedy speaking means losing letters! Squash *I* and *am* together and you get *I'm*. *You* and *will* make *you'll*. *Do* plus *not* make *don't*. Words like this are called **contractions**.

READ the words. FILL IN the blanks with the correct contractions.

Example: you + are = you're

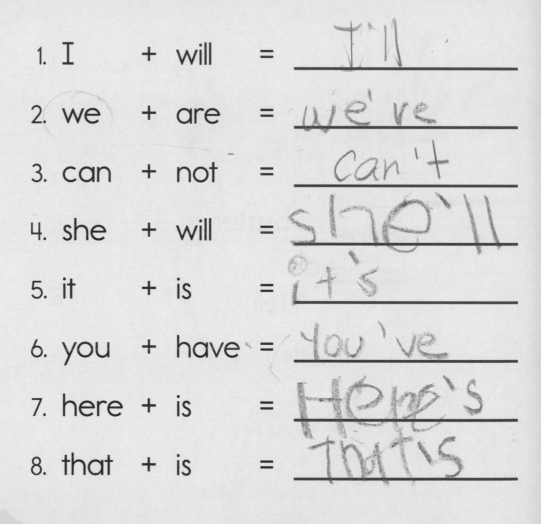

1. I + will = _I'll_

2. we + are = _we're_

3. can + not = _can't_

4. she + will = _she'll_

5. it + is = _it's_

6. you + have = _you've_

7. here + is = _Here's_

8. that + is = _That is_

I'm done!

You've Got Mail

LOOK at the contractions in the word box. FILL IN the blanks with the right ones. You can use each contraction only once.

isn't	I'm	You're	wasn't		who's	what's
Here's	it's	she'll	she's		I'll	

_____ not going to believe me, but _____ true!
₁   ₂

My family is going to the moon! Seriously. _____ the
                                                        ₃

plan: _____ going to build a rocket. Mom knows about
        ₄

engines, so _____ plan that. Guess _____ the
              ₅   ₆

pilot? My sister! I _____ going to bring her, but
                      ₇

_____ the only driver. She says it _____ going
₈   ₉

to work. _____ show her! So, _____ up with you?
          ₁₀   ₁₁

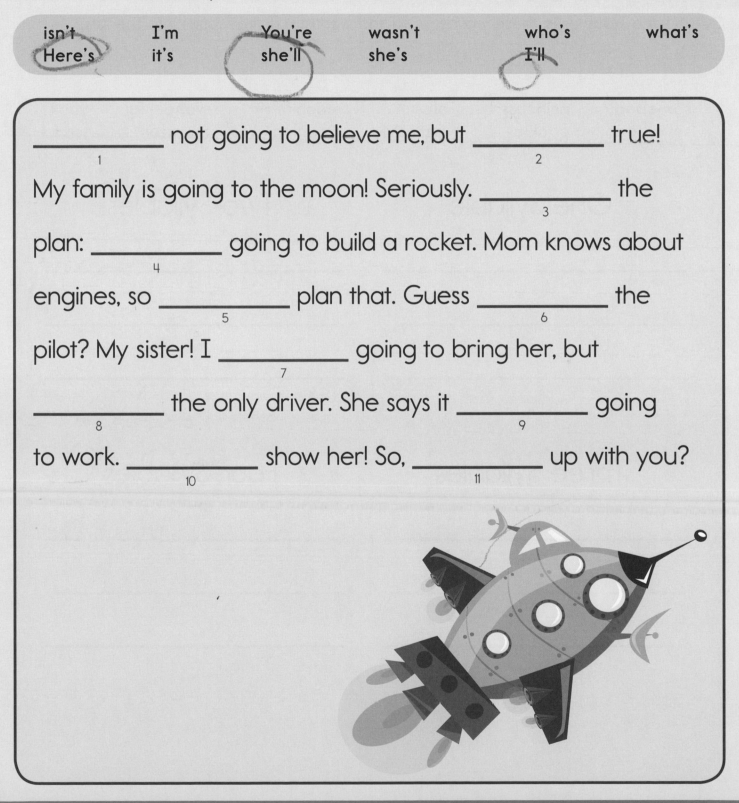

Sort It Out

Pup is a word with one beat. *Puppy* has two beats. These beats are **syllables**. Most of the time, a syllable has a vowel in it.

COUNT the syllables in these words. SORT the words. PUT the words into the lists.

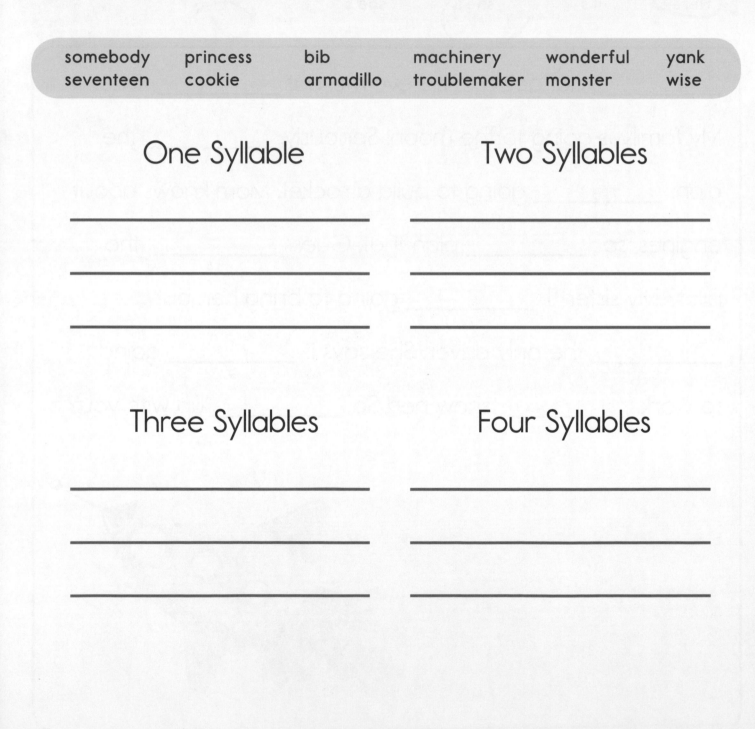

somebody   princess   bib   machinery   wonderful   yank
seventeen   cookie   armadillo   troublemaker   monster   wise

One Syllable

_____

_____

_____

Two Syllables

_____

_____

_____

Three Syllables

_____

_____

_____

Four Syllables

_____

_____

_____

Break It Up

SPLIT each word into syllables. FILL IN the blanks so that a dot sits between each syllable.

1. bulldozer = _____ • _____ • _____

2. crocodile = _____ • _____ • _____

3. fearful = _____ • _____

4. hamster = _____ • _____

5. Apatosaurus = ___ • ___ • ___ • ___

6. chipmunk = _____ • _____

7. Triceratops = ___ • ___ • ___ • ___

8. basketball = _____ • _____ • _____

57

Say Hey!

READ the sentences. FILL IN the blanks with words from the word box.

HINT: Each missing word rhymes with a word next to it—and also has the same number of syllables.

| mother | meter | battle | December | swallowing | alligator |

1. Put the dime in the parking _____, Peter.

2. The monster kept following, _____ people all the way!

3. Your lizard needs to take the _____ elevator.

4. Babies who fight are having a rattle _____.

5. My brother, _____, and father look just like me.

6. I can't remember _____ or January at all.

Herd That Word

Cowgirl Sybil's roping syllables—and she's counting on you!

LOOK at the number next to each fence. READ the words inside the fence. CIRCLE the word that has the correct number of syllables.

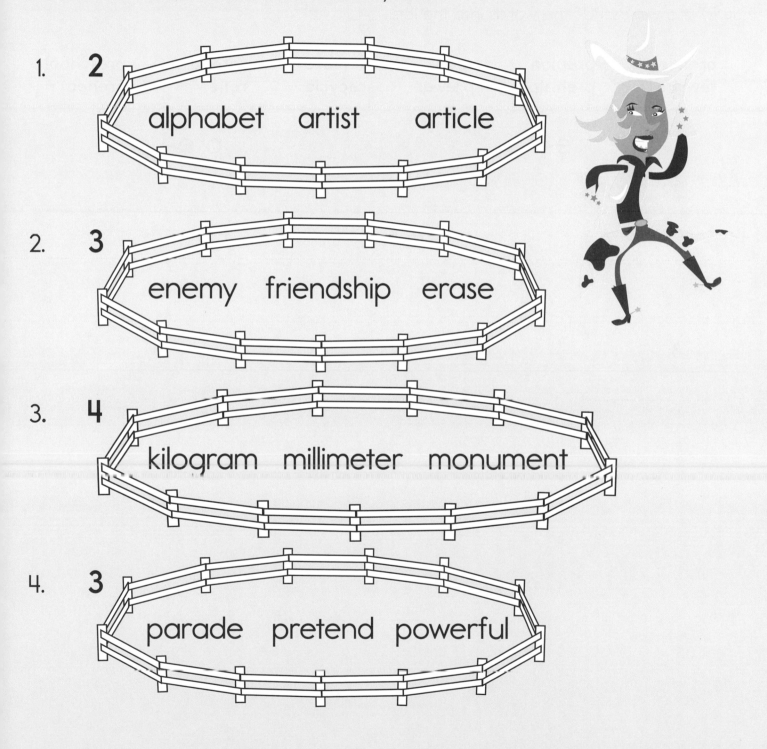

1. **2**

alphabet   artist   article

2. **3**

enemy   friendship   erase

3. **4**

kilogram   millimeter   monument

4. **3**

parade   pretend   powerful

Sort It Out

A **prefix** is a letter or group of letters added to the beginning of a word. It changes a word's meaning. The prefix "re-," for example, means *back* or *again*. The prefix "pre-" means *before*. So *repay* means *pay back* but *prepay* means *pay before*.

SORT the words. PUT the words into the lists.

premix	preplan	redo	remake	reread	preschool
rewrite	prehistory	prewar	recycle	retie	preheat

re-

_____

_____

_____

_____

_____

pre-

_____

_____

_____

_____

_____

Break It Up

"Dis-" and "un-" swap a word's meaning! "Un-" turns *fair* into *unfair.* "Dis-" turns *respect* into *disrespect.* See what happens when you chop off these words' prefixes.

SPLIT each word. FILL IN the blanks with the prefix and the word.

1. unzip = _____ + _____

2. disagree = _____ + _____

3. disobey = _____ + _____

4. unreal = _____ + _____

5. disappear = _____ + _____

6. untie = _____ + _____

7. untidy = _____ + _____

8. dislike = _____ + _____

Build It

It would be a mistake to diss "mis-"! The prefix "mis-" means *bad* or *wrong*.

ADD "mis-" to each word. FILL IN the blanks with the new words.

1. mis + use = _____

2. mis + treat = _____

3. mis + spell = _____

4. mis + lead = _____

5. mis + behave = _____

6. mis + match = _____

7. mis + place = _____

8. mis + understand = _____

Match the Socks

READ the socks. MATCH each sock with another sock. COLOR the socks so they match.

HINT: Socks with prefixes make pairs with socks that have words.

dis-

un-

pre-

re-

visit

lead

obey

history

mis-

fair

Build It

A **suffix** is a letter or group of letters added to the end of a word. A suffix can change a word's meaning a little or a lot. Adding "-er" or "-est," for example, makes *tall* even *taller* until it's the *tallest*.

ADD a suffix to each word. FILL IN the blanks with the new words.

Word	Word + -er	Word + -est
1. slow	_____	_____
2. deep	_____	_____
3. dull	_____	_____
4. short	_____	_____
5. fast	_____	_____
6. gross	_____	_____
7. old	_____	_____
8. smart	_____	_____

Build It

The suffix "-y" changes words so that they describe things. *Dust*, for example, turns into *dusty*. Its buddy "-ly" changes words so that they describe actions. *Glad*, for example, turns into *gladly*.

ADD each word to a suffix. FILL IN the blanks with the new words.

1. quick   + ly = _____

2. mess   + y = _____

3. twist   + y = _____

4. loud   + ly = _____

5. dead   + ly = _____

6. pick   + y = _____

7. strange + ly = _____

8. slink   + y = _____

Herd That Word

Sufferin' suffixes! Cowgirl Inga is at the end of her rope. She needs to round up words ending with the suffixes "-ed" and "-ing," as in *worked* and *working*.

LOOK at the suffix next to each fence. READ the words inside the fence. CIRCLE the word with the suffix on its end.

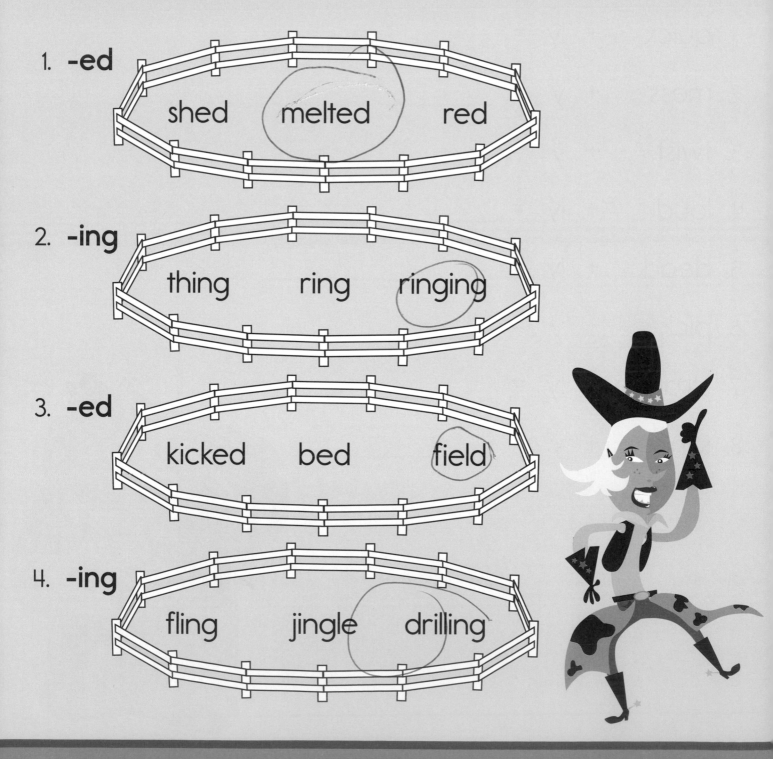

1. **-ed**

   shed   melted   red

2. **-ing**

   thing   ring   ringing

3. **-ed**

   kicked   bed   field

4. **-ing**

   fling   jingle   drilling

You've Got Mail

LOOK at the suffixes in the word box. FILL IN the blanks with the right suffixes. You can use suffixes more than once.

-er	-est	-ed	-ing	-y	-ly

Today will be the weird_____ day ever. We're visit_____

Aunt Rose. She has a very stink_____ pig for a pet. Last time

it chew_____ on my foot. Uncle Al is meet_____ us there.

He's even weird_____ than Aunt Rose. He lives in the world's

dark_____ house. It's creep_____ and awful_____ cold,

too! Strange_____, he hasn't turn_____ on the heat since

1969. Just think_____ about it makes me feel cold_____.

What's It About?

Pick the One!

A nonfiction book or article gives you lots of information about something. That "something" is the **main idea**.

LOOK at each book cover. READ the main ideas listed next to it. CIRCLE the correct main idea.

1.

   a. How balloons are made

   b. How to make balloon animals

   c. Why animals need air

2.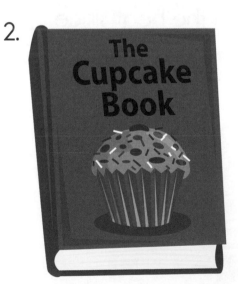

   a. How to bake cupcakes

   b. How to bake anything

   c. Foods of the world

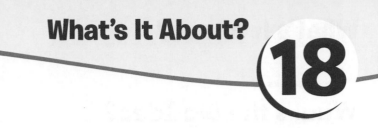
3.

a. How to surf in the sea

b. How to make nets

c. How to use the Internet

4.

a. How to care for your monkey

b. Fun backyard games

c. How to start a zoo

What's It About?

What's the Big Idea?

A book has a main idea. So do smaller bits of writing—even paragraphs!

READ each paragraph. CIRCLE the sentence that sums up its main idea.

1. Do you like to slide on ice? Then you might like the sport of curling. The playing pieces are heavy pots called stones. The players slide the stones across the ice. They clear the stone's path by sweeping the ice with little brooms! They try to get their stones close to a target. The team with the most stones close to the target wins.

What's the main idea?

a. Sliding on ice will curl your hair.

b. Some people sweep ice with little brooms.

c. Curling is a sport played on ice.

2. What kind of bird is a Roc? A Roc looks like a giant eagle—really giant! It's so big, it can pick up ships with its beak. It also likes to drop huge rocks on them. This big bird eats elephants for lunch. Its eggs are as big as a house. Luckily, you won't find it in your backyard! The Roc is found only in old stories.

What's the main idea?

a. Some birds lay eggs as big as houses.

b. The Roc is a very big, strong bird.

c. Old stories are scary.

Sort It Out

Main ideas are fine, but they need **supporting details** or you won't learn much. Check out these details. Which main ideas do they support?

SORT the words. PUT the words into the lists.

pedals	bat	umpire	collar	mitt	tail
leash	brakes	barking	kickstand	pitcher	tires

All About Dogs

_____

_____

_____

_____

How to Play Baseball

_____

_____

_____

_____

Parts of a Bicycle

_____

_____

_____

_____

It's All in the Details

These two kids are writing reports. Both kids have main ideas ready to go. But they need help with the supporting details.

LOOK at each kid's main idea. READ the supporting details. CIRCLE the details that support each kid's main idea. CROSS OUT the ones that don't.

1. Making Cool Flip-Flops

   a. Add flowers.

   b. Glue on glitter.

   c. Socks keep your feet warm.

   d. Color them with markers.

   e. It's fun to paint your toenails.

2. Caring for a Pet Rat

   a. Rats eat cheese.

   b. Owls eat mice.

   c. Rats like to hide.

   d. "Rat" spelled backward is "tar."

   e. You can teach rats tricks.

Teamwork Rules!

READ the paragraph. FILL IN the main idea and details.

People in every country like snacks—but they like different kinds. Some people in Cambodia enjoy fried spiders. Squid-flavored potato chips are a hit in Thailand. Some Canadians snack on crispy seaweed. Roasted ants are yummy in parts of South America. Think these snacks are weird? Try an American favorite—pieces of fried pigskin called pork rinds!

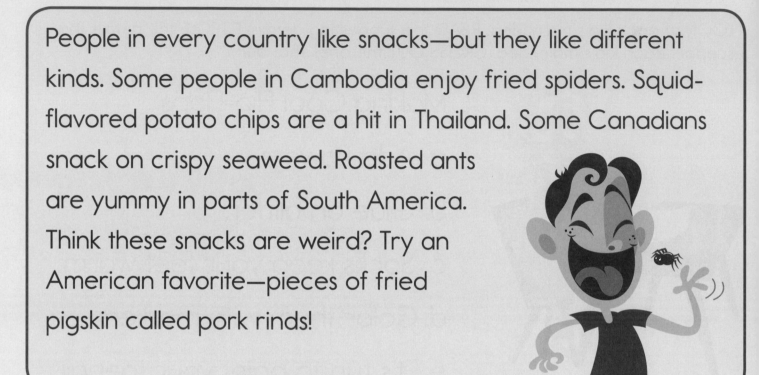

What is the main idea?

_____

_____

List the details.

1. _____   3. _____

2. _____   4. _____

5. _____

Volcanoes make many different kinds of lava. Lava that flows like a river full of sharp chunks of rock is called *aa*. Thin lava that flows fast and far is called *pahoehoe*. Volcanoes also spit out round blobs of lava called bombs. Blobs that are more like boxes are called blocks. Little lava stones are called *lapilli*.

What is the main idea?

_____

_____

List the details.

1. _____

2. _____

3. _____

4. _____

5. _____

Fix-up Mix-up

It's hard to understand what you read if it's all mixed up. The information has to be in the right order. That goes for fiction as well as nonfiction. This correct order is called **sequence**.

LOOK at the sentences and pictures. MATCH the sentences with pictures to put them in the right order.

1.

| Then add yogurt. | Mix them to make a smoothie. | First, put a banana into the blender. |

2.

| A baby bird hatched from the egg. | It laid an egg in the nest. | The bird built a nest. |

3. Mom gave
me one.

I asked for
a haircut.

I'll never ask for
a haircut again!

4. Oops—
it broke!

What a
big mess.

Zoe tied
the garbage
bag shut.

Order Up

Some words help you figure out sequence. Words like *first*, *next*, and *later* help you put things in order. You'll need them to understand this e-mail!

READ the paragraph. LOOK for the words in the word box. PUT the sentences in the right order and FILL IN the blanks.

first	next	then	after

After the ride, I fed him some hay. First, I put a saddle on Blaze. Then, we went over the last jump. Next, I rode into the ring.

1. _____.

2. _____.

3. _____.

4. _____.

Order Up

Now try it with a newspaper article.

READ the article. LOOK for the words in the word box. PUT the sentences in the right order and FILL IN the blanks.

after	finally	first	later	next	then

Rocket Lands on Mars!

After passing the clouds, it zoomed into space. Later, it will leave Mars and go to Jupiter. First, the rocket's engines started. Next, it zipped past the clouds. Finally, it reached Mars. Then the rocket blasted off.

1. _____.

2. _____.

3. _____.

4. _____.

5. _____.

6. _____.

Make a Prediction

Pick the One!

When you think you know what is going to happen, you are making a **prediction**. You can look at a book and **predict** what it's going to be about.

LOOK at the book covers. CIRCLE the prediction that is the best match for each one.

1.

   a. This book tells you how to drive a car.
   b. This book is about a person who is a clown.
   c. This book is about circus elephants.

2.

   a. Dudley gets a great report card.
   b. Dudley teaches you how to play the kazoo.
   c. Everything goes wrong for Dudley.

3.

a. Kia's baseball broke the window. How will she pay for it?

b. Kia hits a record number of home runs! She's the star of Little League!

c. A window fell out of a house and landed right on Kia's baseball!

4.

a. This book is about all the things you can use to stick stuff together.

b. This book is all about bubblegum.

c. This book is about a boy who gets in trouble for chewing gum in class.

What Happens Next?

You can also use your powers of prediction after you start reading a book! READ the story starters. FILL IN the blanks with your predictions.

HINT: Ask yourself, "What happens next?"

1. The police dog sniffed the ground as he ran. He never took his nose off the trail. He was like a vacuum cleaner with legs! Suddenly he stopped. He sniffed harder. Then he began to dig. "What did you find, Sherlock?" said Officer Mya.

Prediction: _Sherlock found gems._

2. Raj heard his cell phone ring. He pulled it out of his pocket. "Hello?" he said. But all he heard was a strange buzzing sound. It grew louder and louder. Then the phone began to shake. It shook so hard, Raj had to let go. The phone shot up into the air—and was sucked into the window of a UFO!

Prediction: _Raj swag and graded it._

3. Count von Looby heated a test tube over a flame. He wrote notes in his notebook. Then he emptied the test tube into a bowl. Sparks flew. A huge cloud of steam filled the air. "Hooray!" he cried, jumping up and down. "It worked! This discovery will change the world!" Just then, he heard a tap at his door.

Prediction: A bad scientist wanted to steal the discovery.

4. The fishermen leaned over the side of the boat. They grabbed the net and pulled with all their might. Finally, they got the net on board. It was full of fish. "What a great catch," said Hal.

"Sure is," said Clyde. "But wait, what's this?"

Hal and Clyde looked closer. Then Hal screamed, "Watch out!"

Prediction: it was a shark Shark.

What Do You See?

Picture This!

You see pictures when you read—even if there are no pictures in the book! That's because you form pictures in your mind. You **visualize** what you're reading.

READ each sentence. CIRCLE the picture that matches it best.

1. The pirate opened the treasure chest, which was filled with gold!

a.   b.   c.

2. A wolf uses her mouth to pick up and carry her cub.

a.   b.   c.

3. Molly's new dress was long and covered with pink dots.

a.   c.

4. Baby Bear was sad because someone ate his porridge.

a.   b.   c.

What Do You See?

Use Your Doodle

You can put the picture in your mind on paper too!

READ each paragraph. DRAW the picture that it makes you visualize.

Everybody knows Australia has kangaroos. But Australia has other strange animals too. One of them is the numbat. It looks like a red squirrel with a long nose and white stripes on its body.

The hairy-nosed wombat is bigger. It looks like a cute, cuddly bear cub crossed with a pig. The quoll looks like a dark brown weasel covered with white spots. Strangest of all is the platypus. It's a furry brown animal with a tail like a beaver's and a bill like a duck's!

The strong wind snatched Jacob's hat off his head. Tumbleweeds raced by. His dog ran in circles around him, barking. "Come on, Chip," he called to the dog. He ducked his head and ran toward the house.

In the distance, he saw the tornado touch the ground. He knew it would reach the farm in less than a minute. Reaching down, he grabbed Chip's collar. He pushed the dog into the storm cellar. Then he jumped in too and pulled the door shut behind him.

Classify This!

Fiction or Not?

Okay, so you can predict what's in a book. You can visualize as you read. It's also important to **classify** what you're reading. You classify it when you decide that it is fiction or nonfiction. Remember: Fiction is made up. Nonfiction is all about facts.

LOOK at the book descriptions. READ the sentences. CLASSIFY the book. CIRCLE your answer.

In *Battle the Sea*, ten-year-old Yin tries to swim across the English Channel. But when a storm hits, she is swept away. Lost at sea, Yin fears she is doomed. Suddenly a seal rescues her. Where will the seal take her? Will she ever see her family again?

1. I think this book is: fiction   nonfiction

Knit Now tells you what you need to know to knit. Find out how to pick the right needles. Learn about different kinds of yarn. See how many different things you can make. Soon you'll be knitting scarves and mittens for your friends!

2. I think this book is: fiction   nonfiction

Clouds of Dust tells the story of a sad time in American history called the Dust Bowl. In the 1930s, land in part of the United States did not get a lot of rain. The soil dried up and blew away. Huge clouds of dust turned the sky black.

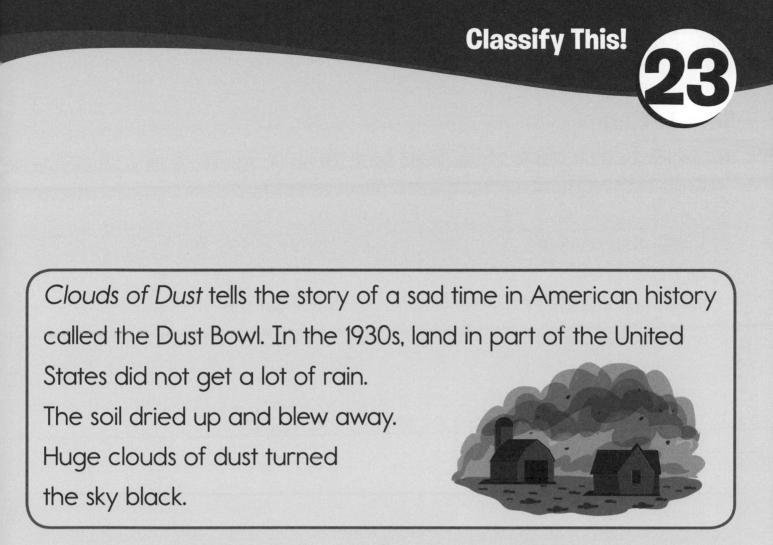

3. I think this book is: fiction   nonfiction

Strike One for Cody is the story of Cody Walsh. He's always been the best hitter on the team. But now he's striking out all the time. Not only that, but he told a lie to his best friend Trey—and now Trey's not talking to him.

4. I think this book is: fiction   nonfiction

Classify This!

Sort It Out

Use your prediction skills to classify these book titles.

SORT the titles. PUT them into the lists.

The Cross-eyed Croc

Be a Babysitter

Peppy Pup and Kitty Kit

Baking for Beginners

How to Speak French

Tessa's First Sleepover

All about Tape

Mystery in the Ballpark

I Predict ... Fiction!

_____

_____

_____

_____

I Predict ... Nonfiction!

_____

_____

_____

_____

Match Up

Librarians classify books all the time. Books that are like each other are put into the same group.

LOOK at the list. CLASSIFY the books by drawing a line from each book to the name of a group.

American fiction

Music

Animals

Math

That's Your Opinion

"Slugs are slimy" is a **fact**. "Slugs are yucky" is an **opinion**. It tells how you feel about the fact that slugs are slimy.

READ the sentences these kids are saying. CIRCLE the facts. UNDERLINE the opinions.

Broccoli is good for you.

Rain boots keep your feet dry.

Electricity is dangerous.

My mom is very strict.

I have a little sister.

Spinach is gross.

Your hair looks funny.

Sneakers are the best shoes in the world.

Herd Those Words

Cowgirl Shirl is after the truth. She wants facts, not opinions!

READ the sentences. CIRCLE the sentence that states a fact.

1. a. Cats are dumb.
    b. Cats have fur.
    c. Cats are the cutest animals.

2. a. Plums are purple.
    b. Purple is an ugly color.
    c. Purple is very cool.

3. a. Football is boring.
    b. Football is a sport.
    c. Football is exciting.

4. a. This soup is awful.
    b. This soup is delicious.
    c. This soup is tomato.

Sort It Out

Writers often use both facts and opinions. See if you can sort them out.

READ the paragraphs. FIND four facts and four opinions. WRITE them in the blanks.

The mayor is putting a new statue in the park. This is a bad idea. It will cost one million dollars. I think that money should be used to fix streets. The streets are full of cracks and potholes. Plus, the statue is really ugly. It's a giant troll. It'll look really bad!

Facts

_____

_____

_____

_____

Opinions

_____

_____

_____

_____

Sort It Out

Let's try another.

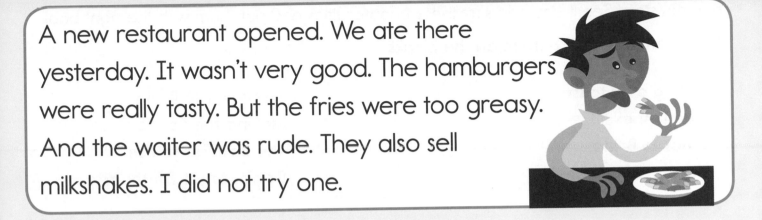

A new restaurant opened. We ate there yesterday. It wasn't very good. The hamburgers were really tasty. But the fries were too greasy. And the waiter was rude. They also sell milkshakes. I did not try one.

Facts

_____

_____

_____

_____

Opinions

_____

_____

_____

Sort It Out

Look in the front of a book, and you may find a **table of contents.** The table of contents tells you what's in the book. It includes chapter titles and page numbers that show where chapters start. See if you can sort these chapter titles and put them with the right book.

SORT the titles. WRITE them on the blanks.

Buying a Suitcase
Side Dishes
What to Bring
How to Choose Noodles

What Not to Bring
Making the Sauce
The Best Pot to Use
Don't Forget Toothpaste

Packing for a Trip

_____

_____

_____

Cooking Spaghetti

_____

_____

_____

Look It Up

Take a look at this table of contents. Use it to answer the questions.

READ the questions. FILL IN the blanks.

1. What chapter tells about toy boats? _____

2. What chapter tells about blocks? _____

3. What chapter tells about radio-controlled planes?

_____

4. What chapter tells about toys from 100 years ago?

_____

What Do You Mean?

Some books have a mini dictionary in them. It's called a **glossary**. The glossary is at the end of the book. It gives you meanings for some words in the book. Try writing one here.

READ the words. FILL IN the blanks with a definition for each one.

A Glossary for *The Book of Food*

banana: _____

_____

carrot: _____

_____

doughnut: _____

_____

hot dog: _____

_____

lemon: _____

_____

Find It Fast

A nonfiction book may have an **index** at the very end. An index is a list of words in alphabetical order. You use it to look up a topic and find out what page it's on.

READ the sentences. LOOK UP the answers in the index. FILL IN the blanks with the page numbers.

1. "Bluebird" is on page _____.
2. "Nests" is on page _____.
3. "Woodpecker" is on page _____.
4. "Flight" is on page _____.
5. "Ovenbird" is on page _____.
6. "Crow" is on page _____.

Index for *The Book of Birds*

bluebird, 21

bluejay, 26

crow, 17

duck, 52

flight, 10

food, 8

goose, 43

nests, 9

ovenbird, 28

woodpecker, 33

wren, 40

As a Matter of Fact

READ the sentences the family is saying. CIRCLE the facts. DRAW A LINE under the opinions.

I think my bedtime is way too early.

It was sunny this morning.

Our class has a new teacher.

This food is disgusting.

The bus got a flat tire on the way to school.

Seth is the funniest person in the world.

Everything tastes better with yams in it.

The cat ate the canary today.

Blank Out

READ the book pages. FILL IN the blanks with words from the list.

glossary	index	table of contents

1. This book part is the _____.

fang: a long, sharp tooth
forked: a tongue that ends in two points
scale: thick patches in a snake's skin
venom: a snake's poison

2. This book part is the _____.

boa, 6
deserts, 24
eggs, 4
fangs, 8
rattlesnake, 13
sidewinder, 5
viper, 17

3. This book part is the _____.

Fiction or Not?

LOOK at the book covers. READ the sentences. CLASSIFY the book. CIRCLE your answer.

1.

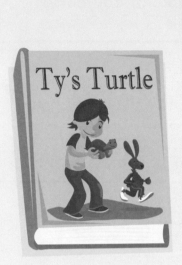

Ty loves his pet turtle, Boo. Boo and Ty like to run races in slow motion in the yard. One sad day, Ty can't find Boo anywhere. He fears that Boo has run away. But why? Does Boo's disappearance have anything to do with the speedy rabbit next door?

I think this book is   fiction   nonfiction

2.

A turtle's body is protected by its shell. Many kinds of turtles can pull their heads, tails, and legs into their shells. The box turtle can even clamp its shell shut after it pulls everything in! This book tells you everything you want to know about turtles.

I think this book is   fiction   nonfiction

Answers

Page 2
br: break, bring, brave
cl: clam, clock, cloud
fl: flip, floppy, flower
gr: grape, green, ground
bl: black, block, blue

Page 3
1. blaze
2. crab
3. frown
4. please

Page 4
1. blouse
2. cloud
3. brave
4. drive
5. floor
6. triangle

Page 5
Wow! Today I flew down a **steep** hill on my **skateboard.** I went so fast the wheels made **smoke.** It was **sweet!** But I had to **slow** down and **spin** sideways when a **skunk** suddenly crawled across the street like a tired **snail** or else it would have made a big **stink. Scary!**

Page 6
1. crabby, crocodile, crayon→Craig
2. spot, spinach, spoon→Spencer
3. snack, snake, snowman→Snowden
4. frog, French, fries→Francis
5. troll, tractor, trouble→Trixie
6. Please, plant, plate→Placido

Page 7
France, sleep, creepy, dragon, prowled, crushed, claws, broke, branches, trees, breath, fried, grass, problem, tried, trap, prince, flew, scared, grinning, spider, ground, pretty, great

Page 8
A really **strange** thing happened today. I was eating a bowl of **strawberry** ice cream when I heard a loud **screech.** Then I heard a **squeak** and a **squawk.** I jumped up to look out the window and saw a noisy **struggle** going on between a **squirrel** and a bird. They were playing tug-of-war with a **string!** Suddenly the bird let go. The squirrel fell into the **stream** with a **splash.** I sat down in surprise. Whoops. I **squashed** my ice cream—and let out a **scream!**

Page 9
spr: spray, spread, spring
squ: square, squash, squirm
spl: split, splat, splash
scr: screech, scram, scream
str: strike, street, stripe

Page 10
1. shelf
2. jump
3. want
4. left

Page 11
1. wind, and, sand→Desmond
2. Honk, pink, tank→Hank
3. aunt, went, sent→Millicent
4. jump, ramp, swamp→Kemp
5. best, west, fast→Amethyst
6. Ask, task, tusk→Fisk

Page 12
1. breakfast
2. soft
3. sent
4. felt
5. sunk
6. swamp
Note: "sump" and "swank" are also possbile answers to 5 and 6.

Page 13
1. lamp
2. ant
3. desk
4. elf

Page 14
1. She, shells, shore→Sheila
2. chubby, chicken, cheese→Chuck
3. think, thousand, things→Theo
4. white, whale, Whatever→Whitney
5. threw, three, through→Thrasher

Page 15
1. cheese
2. wheel
3. thunder
4. thread
5. shark

Page 16
1. laugh
2. thing
3. sting
4. cough

Page 17
1. rough
2. sting
3. laugh
4. song
5. rang
6. tough

Page 18
Hard c: cat, cave, cold, cobwebs, canary
Soft c: Cinnamon, ceiling, Centipedes, center, circle

Page 19
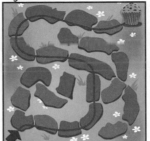

Page 20
Hard g: gab, goat, girl, game, garden, gobble
Soft g: gentle, general, germ, ginger, giraffe, giant

Page 21
1. gorilla
2. gym
3. gift
4. ginger

Page 22
kn: knees, know
wr: wrong, wreck
mb: crumb, lamb

Page 23
1. knight
2. comb
3. writer
4. knee

Page 24
1. cute
2. dime
3. fine
4. fire
5. kite
6. made
7. pine
8. plane

Page 25
mole, nose, fine, came, hate, shade, pine, lake, shape, plane, kite, time, hide, dive, hole, rude, mule, joke

Page 26
1. gray
2. play
3. way
4. rain
5. pain
6. jail
7. wail
8. pails
9. eight

Page 27

Page 28
1. seal
2. me
3. neat
4. sheep
5. honey
6. sneak

Page 29
1. bean
2. flee
3. he
4. monkey

Page 30
ie: lie, cried, pie, tie
igh: light, high, night, fight
y: sky, fly, cry, my

Page 31
night, pie, sky, light, high, my, delight, sighed, fly, sly, cried, try

Page 32
1. bone
2. coat
3. crow
4. go

Page 33
1. boat
2. holes
3. gold
4. slow
5. cold
6. cocoa
7. soap
8. potatoes
9. toast

Page 34
1. mule
2. stew
3. glue
4. juice

Page 35
1. blue
2. flu
3. unicorn
4. juice
5. knew
6. new

Answers

Page 36
er: dinner, germ, herd, paper
ir: bird, dirt, first, girl
ur: burp, curl, fur, turn

Page 37
Bird, Turtle, dinner, purple, silver,
manners, stirred, germs, her, dirty,
burp, Surprise, spider, first, birthday

Page 38
1. award
2. horse
3. core
4. four

Page 39
1. fork
2. bored
3. award
4. pour
5. torn
6. wart

Page 40
1. hair
2. stare
3. pear
4. care

Page 41
1. bear
2. hair
3. stare
4. care
5. pair
6. underwear
7. fair
8. bare

Page 42
1. toys
2. oil
3. oyster
4. noise
5. soil
6. boy

Page 43
1. boy
2. noise
3. oil
4. toy

Page 44
1. town
2. mouse
3. fowl
4. mouth

Page 45
Wow, brown, hound, fountain, found,
Trout, mouth, crouched, pounced,
howled, drown, Cow, loud, sounds,
mouse, out, chow, now

Page 46
Goo oo: boot, cool, food, poodle,
school, tooth
Good oo: cook, foot, wood, hook,
look, took

Page 47
1. room
2. zoom
3. goose
4. moose
5. drool
6. food
7. books
8. good
9. zoo
10. Shoo

Page 48
1. ball
2. yawn
3. hawk
4. chalk

Page 49
1. bawl
2. dawn
3. wall
4. small
5. talk
6. claws

Page 50
1. bulldog
2. snowman
3. blackberry
4. cupcake
5. gingerbread
6. newspaper
7. popcorn
8. bathroom

Page 51
1. day + light
2. rail + road
3. tooth + brush
4. skate + board
5. pine + cone
6. base + ball
7. suit + case
8. star + fish

Page 52

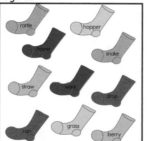

Page 53
1. jellyfish
2. butterfly
3. sidewalk
4. scarecrow
5. toothpaste
6. cupcake

Page 54
1. I'll
2. we're
3. can't
4. she'll
5. it's
6. you've
7. here's
8. that's

Page 55
1. You're
2. it's
3. Here's
4. I'm
5. she'll
6. who's
7. wasn't
8. she's
9. isn't
10. I'll
11. what's

Page 56
One Syllable: bib, wise, yank
Two Syllables: cookie, monster,
princess
Three Syllables: seventeen,
somebody, wonderful
Four Syllables: armadillo, machinery,
troublemaker

Page 57
1. bull · doz · er
2. croc · o · dile
3. fear · ful
4. ham · ster
5. A · pat · o · saur · us
6. chip · munk
7. Tri · cer · a · tops
8. bas · ket · ball

Page 58
1. meter
2. swallowing
3. alligator
4. battle
5. mother
6. December

Page 59
1. artist
2. enemy
3. millimeter
4. powerful

Page 60
re-: recycle, redo, remake, reread,
retie, rewrite
pre-: preheat, prehistory, premix,
preplan, preschool, prewar

Page 61
1. un + zip
2. dis + agree
3. dis + obey
4. un + real
5. dis + appear
6. un + tie
7. un + tidy
8. dis + like

Page 62
1. misuse
2. mistreat
3. misspell
4. mislead
5. misbehave
6. mismatch
7. misplace
8. misunderstand

Page 63

Page 64
1. slow slower slowest
2. deep deeper deepest
3. dull duller dullest
4. short shorter shortest
5. fast faster fastest
6. gross grosser grossest
7. old older oldest
8. smart smarter smartest

Page 65
1. quickly
2. messy
3. twisty
4. loudly
5. deadly
6. picky
7. strangely
8. stinky

Page 66
1. melted
2. ringing
3. kicked
4. drilling

Page 67
Today will be the **weirdest** day ever.
We're **visiting** Aunt Rose. She has a
very **stinky** pig for a pet. Last time
it **chewed** on my foot. Uncle Al is
meeting us there. He's even **weirder**
than Aunt Rose. He lives in the
world's **darkest** house. It's **creepy**
and **awfully** cold, too! **Strangely,**
he hasn't **turned** on the heat since
1969. Just **thinking** about it makes
me feel **colder.**

Pages 68–69
1. b
2. a
3. c
4. b

Pages 70–71
1. c
2. b

Page 72
All About Dogs: collar, tail, leash, barking
How to Play Baseball: bat. mitt, umpire, pitcher
Parts of a Bicycle: pedals, tires, brakes, kickstand

Page 73
1. Making Cool Flip-Flops
a. Add flowers.
b. Glue on glitter.
c. Socks keep your feet warm.
d. Color them with markers.
e. It's fun to paint your toenails.

2. Caring for a Pet Rat
a. Rats eat cheese.
b. Owls eat mice.
c. Rats like to hide.
d. "Rat" spelled backward is "tar."
e. You can teach rats tricks.

Page 74
Suggestions:
Main Idea: People eat different snacks in different countries.
Details: 1. fried spiders, 2. squid-flavored potato chips, 3. seaweed, 4. roasted ants, 5. pork rinds

Page 75
Suggestions:
Main Idea: There are different kinds of lava.
Details: 1. aa, 2. pahoehoe, 3. bombs, 4. blocks, 5. lapilli

Page 76

Page 77

Page 78
1. First, I put a saddle on Blaze.
2. Next, I rode into the ring.
3. Then, we went over the last jump.
4. After the ride, I fed him some hay.

Page 79
1. First, the rocket's engines started.
2. Then the rocket blasted off.
3. Next, it zipped past the clouds.
4. After passing the clouds, it zoomed into space.
5. Finally, it reached Mars.
6. Later, it will leave Mars and go to Jupiter.

Pages 80–81
1. b
2. c
3. a
4. b

Pages 82–83
Suggestions:
1. Sherlock finds something that was dropped by the person he is tracking and will soon find the person.
2. Raj will be taken aboard the UFO and will meet space aliens.
3. Count von Looby will open the door and find his neighbor there, who asks him to please keep the noise down.
4. Hal and Clyde discover that they have caught a huge sea monster.

Pages 84–85
1. c
2. a
3. c
4. b

Pages 86–87
Be sure the pictures match something from the paragraphs.

Pages 88–89
1. fiction
2. nonfiction
3. nonfiction
4. fiction

Page 90
Fiction: The Cross-eyed Croc, Peppy Pup and Kitty Kit, Tessa's First Sleepover, Mystery in the Ballpark
Nonfiction: Be a Babysitter, Baking for Beginners, How to Speak French, All about Tape

Page 91
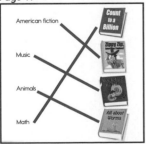

Page 92
Facts
Broccoli is good for you.
Rain boots keep your feet dry.
Electricity is dangerous.
I have a little sister.
Opinions
Spinach is gross.
Sneakers are the best shoes in the world.
Your hair looks funny.
My mom is very strict.

Page 93
1. b
2. a
3. b
4. c

Page 94
Facts
1. The mayor is putting a new statue in the park.
2. It will cost one million dollars.
3. The streets are full of cracks and potholes.
4. It's a giant troll.
Opinions
1. This is a bad idea.
2. I think that money should be used to fix streets.
3. Plus, the statue is really ugly.
4. It'll look really bad.

Page 95
Facts
1. A new restaurant opened.
2. We ate there yesterday.
3. They also sell milkshakes.
4. I did not try one.
Opinions
1. It wasn't very good.
2. The hamburgers were really tasty.
3. But the fries were too greasy.
4. And the waiter was rude.

Page 96
Packing for a Trip: Buying a Suitcase, What to Bring, What Not to Bring, Don't Forget Toothpaste
Cooking Spaghetti: How to Choose Noodles, Making the Sauce, The Best Pot to Use, Side Dishes

Page 97
1. 4
2. 6
3. 3
4. 1

Page 98
Suggestions:
Banana: long yellow fruit with a peel that gets black spots if you leave it lying around for too long
Carrot: an orange vegetable that rabbits like a lot
Doughnut: a circle of dough around a hole
Hot dog: meat shaped like a tube that you put mustard on
Lemon: a sour yellow fruit about the size of a baseball

Page 99
1. 21
2. 9
3. 33
4. 10
5. 28
6. 17

Page 100
Facts
It was sunny this morning.
Our class has a new teacher.
The cat ate the canary today.
The bus got a flat tire on the way to school.
Opinions
Seth is the funniest person in the world.
This food is disgusting.
I think my bedtime is way too early.
Everything tastes better with yams in it.

Page 101
1. table of contents
2. glossary
3. index

Page 102
1. fiction
2. nonfiction

2nd Grade Spelling Games & Activities

Spell Short Vowels

Puzzle Pairs

FILL IN the two different missing vowels in the word pairs to finish the riddles.

1. This beetle was not small.

   He was a **b__g b__g**.

2. When I left my cap on the stove, I had a **h__t h__t**.

3. I did not sleep well last night. I was on a **b__d b__d**.

4. To get pecans out of the tree,

   I used a **n__t n__t**.

5. The rabbit went **h__p h__p** all

   the way up the hill.

Criss Cross

READ the clues. FILL IN the boxes with the right word for each clue.

Across

1. This says "meow."
3. You clean the floor with this.
6. My cat or my dog is my ____.
8. A hole in the ground
10. "You are it!" in the game of ____
11. You sleep here.

Down

2. The highest spot
4. A young dog
5. You ____ a ball with a bat.
7. Wash up in the bath____.
9. One after nine.

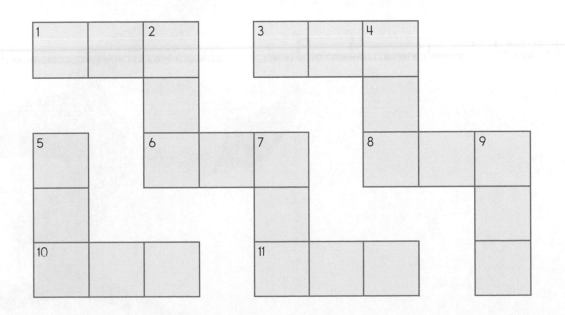

Spell Final E Long Vowels

Puzzle Pairs

FILL IN the missing vowels in the word pairs to finish the sentences. Listen for how the final "-e" changes the vowel sound.

1. When it's my turn,

   I **h__p__** I can **h__p**.

2. My sister broke my toy. It **m__d__** me **m__d**.

3. Pete is my dog. If you want, you can **p__t P__t__**.

4. Maya went to the salon and got a **c__t__ c__t**.

5. The shark was a star.

   He had a **f__n__ f__n**.

Not Quite!

CIRCLE the words that are misspelled in this story.

I saw a very cut kitten. I gav him a pok. That mad him hid from me. I hat when that happens! I hop I see him again some tim.

WRITE the circled words correctly.

1. _____

2. _____

3. _____

4. _____

5. _____

6. _____

7. _____

8. _____

Beginning Consonant Combos

Blank Out

FILL IN the missing "ch," "sh," "wh," or "th" in these sentences.

SPELLING LIST

chat

chick

chop

shapes

ship

shop

shut

thick

thin

what

when

white

1. Miguel was _____**ite** as a ghost!

2. I always cry when I _____**op** onions.

3. Yay! Mom gave me a _____**ick** slice of cake!

4. Tom helps his dad _____**op** for food.

5. I want to hear about your day.

   Let's have a little _____**at**.

6. Bella went for a cruise on a _____**ip**.

7. Grandma always feeds me too much.

   She says I look _____**in**.

8. Close the washer door _____**en**

   you wash your clothes.

Match Up

DRAW a line to the correct word ending.

1. **ch**

en   ick

2. **wh**

ite   ig

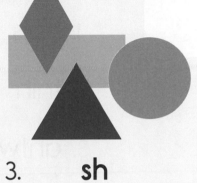

3. **sh**

apes   ogs

4. **sh**

ig   ip

5. **ch**

an   op

6. **sh**

op   ug

Beginning Consonant Combos

Word Scramble

UNSCRAMBLE each word and write it correctly. LOOK at the word box for help.
CROSS OUT each word as you make it.

| thin | thick | chop | chick | chat | shop | ship | shapes | what | white |

1. hpis _____

2. tnih _____

3. ahtw _____

4. kichc _____

5. ithew _____

6. ohpc _____

7. thac _____

8. spesah _____

9. citkh _____

10. psoh _____

Riddle Me This!

UNSCRAMBLE the words in the riddles.

1. **Q.** Why did the bookworm start eating the dictionary at T?

   A. He wanted to eat through **chitk** and **inht**.

   _____   _____

2. **Q.** What do you call talking while eggs hatch?

   A. A **ccikh thca**.

   _____   _____

3. **Q.** Why did the captain build his house like a boat?

   A. He liked things **isph aphes**.

   _____   _____

Ending Consonant Combos

Blank Out!

FILL IN the missing "th," "sh," "ch," or "tch" in these sentences.

SPELLING LIST

bath

math

with

dash

fish

rich

which

catch

watch

witch

1. Johnny ate **fi**_____ sticks for lunch.

2. Come **wi**_____ me to the fair.

3. Tim wondered **whi**_____ way to go.

4. My **wa**_____ says it's five-thirty.

5. Julie was the winner of the 100-yard **da**_____.

6. I like numbers, so **ma**_____ is fun for me.

7. Becky put on her **wi**_____ costume for the party.

8. Kim didn't think she'd **ca**_____ such a big fish!

4

Word Split

DRAW lines to connect word beginnings with the correct endings.

1.  **ba**

 **ch**

2.  **ri**

 **sh**

3.  **ca**

 **th**

4.  **da**

 **tch**

Ending Consonant Combos

Word Blocks

FILL IN the word blocks with words of the same shape from the word box. Use the pictures as clues.

rich	fish	bath	math	witch	watch

1.

2.

3.

4.

5.

6.

Not Quite!

CIRCLE the words that are misspelled in this story.

Sam caught a fish, whish made him happy.

"I am really a wich," it said. "Throw me back, and I will make you ritsh."

"But I might not catsh another fish," said Sam.

"You can buy another one," said the fich. "Come on! Do the maf!"

Sam ate him wif a datsh of salt.

WRITE the circled words correctly.

1. _____

2. _____

3. _____

4. _____

5. _____

6. _____

7. _____

8. _____

Spell Clothing

Word Scramble

UNSCRAMBLE each word and write it correctly. LOOK at the word box for help.
CROSS OUT each word in the word box as you make it.

belt	coat	dress	pants	shirt	shorts	skirt	shoe

SPELLING LIST

belt
coat
dress
pants
shirt
shoe
shorts
skirt

1. sreds _____

2. tisrk _____

3. strih _____

4. atoc _____

5. hoes _____

6. elbt _____

7. rhtoss _____

8. snapt _____

Word Hunt

CIRCLE the words from the word box in the grid. Words go down and across, not diagonally or backward.

belt   coat   dress   pants   shirt   shorts   skirt   shoe

WRITE each word that you circled.

belt.   pants

coat.   shirt.

dress.   shorts.

shoe.   skirt.

Beginning Consonant Blends

Knock Out

CROSS OUT the pictures whose words **don't** begin with two consonant sounds together.

SPELLING
LIST

clam

crab

frog

slide

slip

spill

steps

stick

stop

trap

trip

truck

WRITE the words for the pictures you didn't cross out.

_____   _____

_____   _____

Blank Out

FILL IN the missing letters for each word.

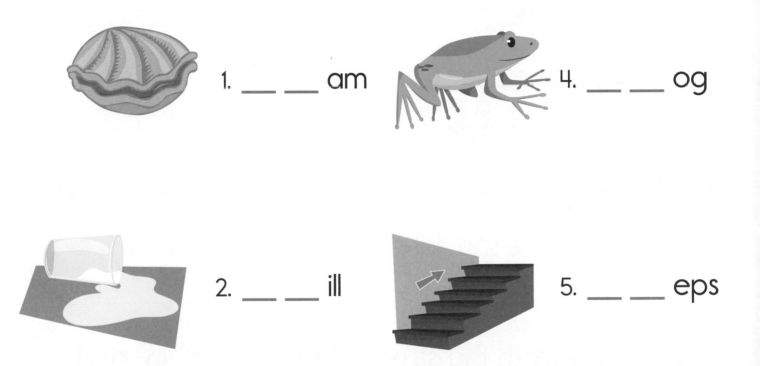

1. __ __ am

4. __ __ og

2. __ __ ill

5. __ __ eps

3. __ __ ap

6. __ __ ab

Beginning Consonant Blends

Puzzle Pairs

FILL IN the missing letters in the word pairs to finish these sentences.

1. The firefighters **tuck** their shirts in before they get on the **t_uck**.

2. The **fog** was so thick at the pond I couldn't even see a **f_og** jump.

3. I felt **sick** about breaking grandpa's walking **s_ick**.

4. **Tap** him on the shoulder and warn him. This is a **t_ap**.

5. Take a **sip** from the stream, but don't **s_ip** and fall in!

6. I took a **cab** to the beach, where I saw a **c_ab**.

7. Chang peeked over the **side** before he went down the **s_ide**.

8. Here's a **tip**: Be careful not to **t_ip**.

Word Scramble

UNSCRAMBLE the words. LOOK at the word box for help. CROSS OUT each word in the word box as you make it.

| clam | frog | slide | stick | steps | trip |
| crab | slip | spill | stop | truck | trap |

1. ipsl _____

2. rtpa _____

3. pesst _____

4. amlc _____

5. skict _____

6. barc _____

7. ospt _____

8. lispl _____

9. ilsed _____

10. prit _____

11. orgf _____

12. urckt _____

Blank Out

FILL IN the missing pair of letters at the end of each word.

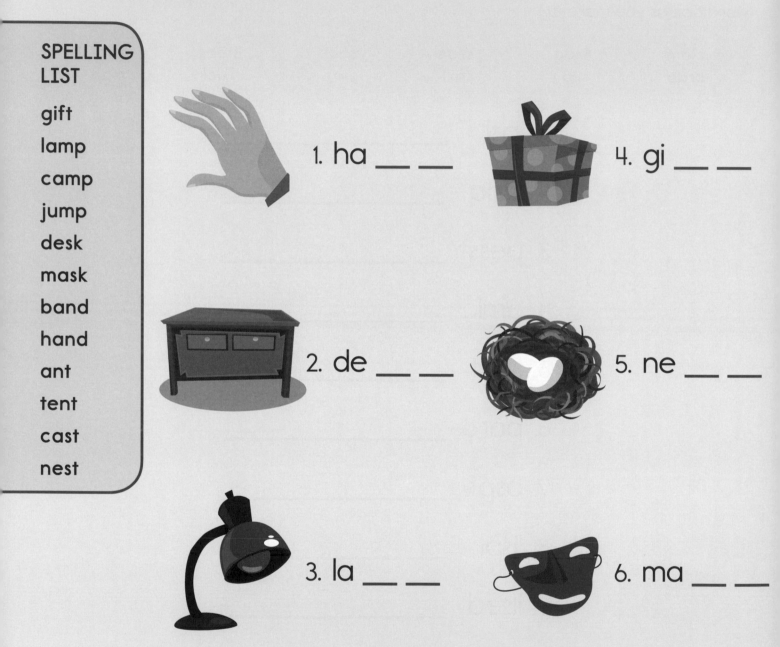

SPELLING LIST

gift

lamp

camp

jump

desk

mask

band

hand

ant

tent

cast

nest

1. ha __ __

2. de __ __

3. la __ __

4. gi __ __

5. ne __ __

6. ma __ __

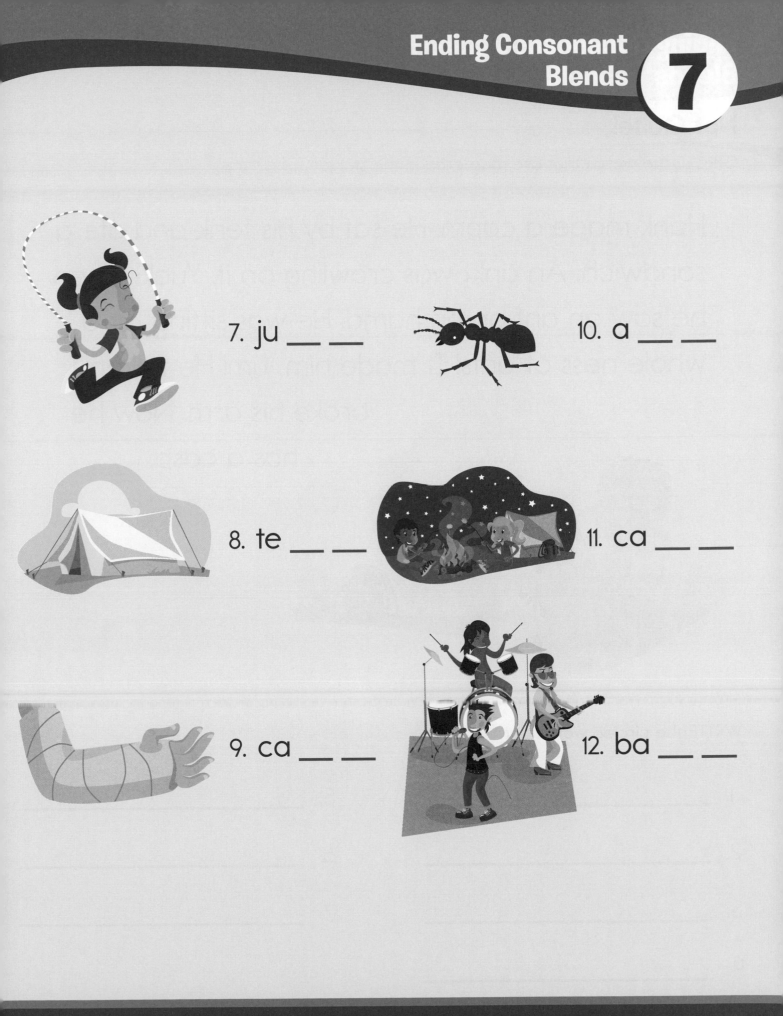

7. ju __ __

10. a __ __

8. te __ __

11. ca __ __

9. ca __ __

12. ba __ __

Ending Consonant Blends

Not Quite!

CIRCLE the words that are misspelled in this story.

Hank made a capm. He sat by his tenk and ate a sandwich. An ankt was crawling on it. Yuck! Then he saw an ant on his hamd. He was sitting on a whole ness of ants! It made him jum! He fell and broke his arm. Now he has a casp.

WRITE the circled words correctly.

1. _____

2. _____

3. _____

4. _____

5. _____

6. _____

7. _____

Word Hunt

CIRCLE the words from the word box in the grid. Words go down and across, not diagonally or backward.

| apple | bread | banana | carrot | cookie | milk | pizza | steak |

```
b r e a d a n s
i b c a r r o t
z a o p p a z e
z n o p i z z a
a a k l m i l k
b n i e p p i d
b a e i l k p p
```

WRITE each word that you circled.

_____   _____

_____   _____

_____   _____

Vowels with "R"

Puzzle Pairs

ADD an "r" to the vowel in each word pair to finish the sentence.

SPELLING
LIST

card

chart

hard

part

her

chirp

first

skirt

bird

worm

hurt

turn

1. Don't **pat** Carlos on the head. It will mess

up the _____ in his hair.

2. That baby bird is a **chip** off the old block.

He can _____ like a champ.

3. In the **skit**, Jayla had to wear an

ugly _____.

4. I bumped my head going into the **hut**.

Boy, did it _____!

5. How do you punch? Making a **fist** is the

_____ step.

6. Brit **bid** on an old painting with a

_____ in a nest.

7. Dion had a **chat** with the mapmaker, who

showed him his best _____.

Herd a Word

WRITE each word from the Spelling List next to the word with the same vowel sound.

girl _____

_____

_____

_____

_____

_____

_____

car _____

_____

_____

_____

Vowels with "R"

Word Scramble

UNSCRAMBLE the words. LOOK at the word box for help. CROSS OUT each word in the word box as you make it.

card hard chart part her first chirp bird skirt worm hurt turn

1. drac _____

2. rathc _____

3. adhr _____

4. ridb _____

5. romw _____

6. trifs _____

7. urnt _____

8. thru _____

9. kitrs _____

10. aprt _____

11. criph _____

12. rhe _____

Which Is Which?

FILL IN the missing letters in this e mail.

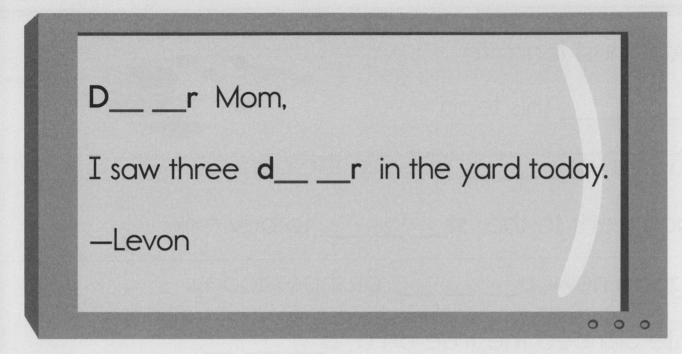

D__ __r Mom,

I saw three **d__ __r** in the yard today.

—Levon

Blank Out

FILL IN the missing "ee" or "ea" in these sentences.

1. Peggy had too much **g__ __r** when she went camping.

2. I gave her some ice cream to **ch__ __r** her up

3. It's hard to **st__ __r** in this driving game.

4. Martha's grandmother was very **d__ __r** to her.

5. Don't go too **n__ __r** that barking dog.

More Vowels with "R"

Blank Out

FILL IN the missing "air," "are," or "ore" in each word.

1. Thad must learn to

   sh__ __ __ his food.

2. Do you **c**__ __ __ if I skip the game?

3. Zach went to the **st**__ __ __ to buy milk.

4. I got a new **p**__ __ __ of shoes today.

5. Kate climbed the tree on a **d**__ __ __.

6. Please stay in your **ch**__ __ __ during dinner.

7. Oliver asked for **m**__ __ __ food.

8. Tanya likes to admire her **h**__ __ __.

Word Scramble

UNSCRAMBLE each word and write it correctly. LOOK at the word box for help.
CROSS OUT each word in the word box as you make it.

| more | store | cheer | steer | gear | near | dare | share | chair | pair |

1. apir _____

2. ehrec _____

3. reag _____

4. eanr _____

5. hraic _____

6. tesre _____

7. remo _____

8. eard _____

9. hreas _____

10. orste _____

What's the Weather?

Word Hunt

CIRCLE the words from the Spelling List in the grid. Words go across and down, not diagonally or backward.

SPELLING LIST

cloud

cold

rain

shower

snow

warm

weather

wind

```
w e a t c w e r
a o u d r a i n
r a w e i r s c
s h o c n m h l
n c l o u d o o
o n d l i n w u
w i n d d w e r
w e a t h e r m
```

WRITE each word that you circled.

_____   _____

_____   _____

_____   _____

_____

Word Scramble

UNSCRAMBLE each word and write it correctly. LOOK at the Spelling List for help.

1. ianr ____________________
2. wamr ____________________
3. ocdl ____________________
4. dniw ____________________
5. rwheeat ____________________
6. ludco ____________________
7. shwoer ____________________
8. nswo ____________________

The Long "A" Way

Sort and Spell

LISTEN for the long **a** sound in each word pictured. DRAW a line from the picture to the box that shows how long **a** is spelled. WRITE the word correctly in the box.

SPELLING LIST

gray
play
say
tray
braid
mail
paint
snail
train
weigh
weight
neighbor

gray   paint   play   snail   train   tray

ay	ai

Knock Out

CROSS OUT the pictures that show words **without** the long **a** sound.

WRITE the words for the pictures you didn't cross out.

_____   _____

_____   _____

The Long "A" Way

Blank Out

FILL IN the missing words in these sentences. LOOK at the word box for help.

| say | play | gray | train | mail | paint | weigh | neighbor |

1. Shen checked the _____ every day for a letter from his friend.

2. I get on the scale to see how much I _____.

3. Stella's dad takes the _____ to work.

4. Penn wants to _____ his room blue so it feels like the ocean.

5. Sometimes I don't know what to _____ when I meet someone new.

6. Janice likes to _____ on the monkey bars.

7. Tad went next door to meet the new _____.

8. The elephant has tough, _____ skin.

Not Quite!

CIRCLE the words that are misspelled in this story.

I went out to plai. My nayber was checking her mayl. She's kind of old, with gra hair—a lot of hair! She has the biggest brade I ever saw. It must wey a ton. She said, "If I roll up this braid, my head will look like a giant snale!" What do you sae to that?

WRITE the circled words correctly.

1. _____

2. _____

3. _____

4. _____

5. _____

6. _____

7. _____

8. _____

Free with Long "E"

Sort and Spell

LISTEN for the long **e** sound in each word pictured. DRAW a line from the picture to the box that shows how long **e** is spelled. WRITE the word in the box.

SPELLING LIST

green
teeth
tree
wheel
beach
leaf
seal
speak
key
monkey
candy
puppy

beach   green   leaf   seal   teeth   wheel

ea

ee

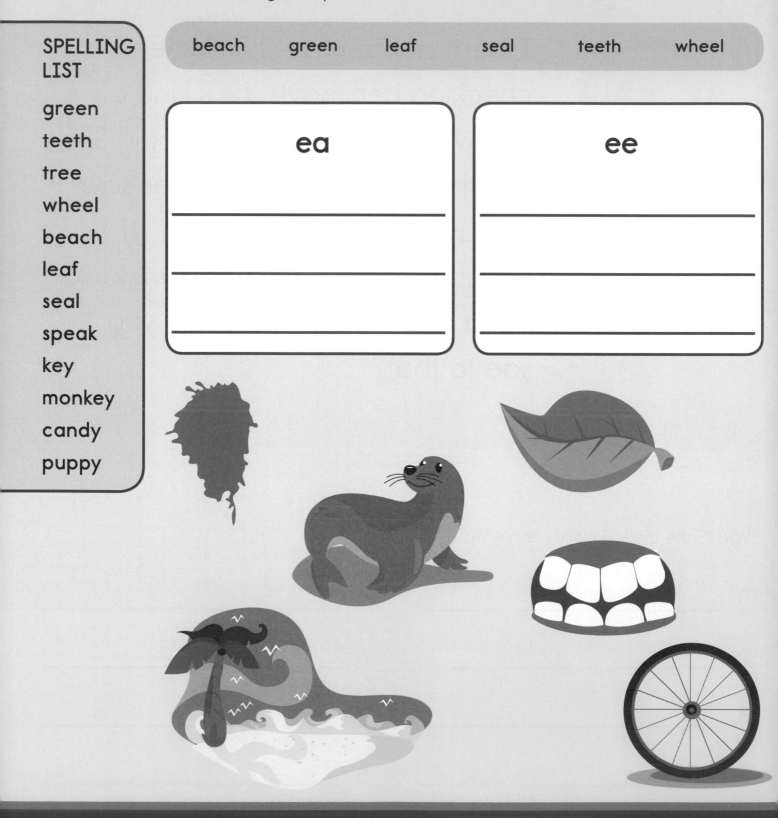

Riddle Me This!

UNSCRAMBLE the words in the riddles. LOOK at the Spelling List for help.

1. **Q.** What did the dentist say when the **acnyd**-loving **pppyu** showed him her **eteth**?

   _____   _____

   _____

   A. Your bite is worse than your bark.

2. **Q.** A **nmeyok** saw a Spanish sparrow and a French hen in a **rete**. What language did he **eapks**?

   _____   _____

   _____

   A. None. Monkeys can't talk.

Knock Out

CROSS OUT the pictures whose words **don't** have a long **e** sound.

WRITE the words for the pictures you didn't cross out.

_____   _____

_____   _____

Word Scramble

UNSCRAMBLE each word and write it correctly. LOOK at the word box for help.
CROSS OUT each word in the word box as you make it.

| green | teeth | wheel | beach | leaf | seal | speak | key | monkey | puppy |

1. eelhw _____

2. abche _____

3. slae _____

4. tthee _____

5. mekoyn _____

6. ngree _____

7. kye _____

8. pupyp _____

9. elfa _____

10. ksepa _____

Try Long "I"

Blank Out

FILL IN the missing "i," "igh," or "y" in these sentences.

SPELLING LIST

blind
find
kind
mind
fly
spy
try
bright
high
light
right
sigh

1. What **k___nd** of sandwich do you want?

2. Joel was singing "Three **bl___nd** mice."

3. I know I hate eggplant, so I don't need to **tr___** it.

4. Sierra's bad mood made her mother **s_____**.

5. The cookies are too **h_____** up for me to reach.

6. Taye hid so well they couldn't **f___nd** him.

7. Jay was so **l_____t** I could lift him easily.

8. The sun is too **br_____t** for me to keep sleeping.

Riddle Me This!

UNSCRAMBLE the words in the riddles. LOOK at the Spelling List for help.

1. **Q.** What do you call a desk lamp that gets straight As?

   A. A **bhgitr htigl**.

   _____ _____

2. **Q.** Why did the crazy guy keep turning left?

   A. He wasn't in his **girth nimd**.

   _____ _____

3. **Q.** What has six legs, wings, and buzzes in code?

   A. A **lfy yps**.

   _____ _____

Try Long "I"

Word Hunt

CIRCLE the words from the word box in the grid. Words go down and across, not diagonally or backward.

| blind | bright | fly | high | kind | light | mind | try |

```
s  f  l  y  i  t  e
b  r  i  g  h  t  n
h  i  g  i  n  r  d
i  f  h  y  k  y  g
g  t  t  g  i  h  s
h  b  l  i  n  d  p
s  m  i  n  d  i  o
```

WRITE each word that you circled.

_____   _____

_____   _____

_____   _____

Word Scramble

UNSCRAMBLE each word and write it correctly. LOOK at the word box for help.
CROSS OUT each word in the word box as you make it.

| blind | find | kind | mind | spy | bright | high | light | right | sigh |

1. dkin _____

2. fidn _____

3. mnid _____

4. ihhg _____

5. inbdl _____

6. rthibg _____

7. pys _____

8. igrht _____

9. ithlg _____

10. gshi _____

The Long "O" Show

Sort and Spell

LISTEN for the long **o** sound in each word pictured. DRAW a line from the picture to the correct sound box. WRITE the word in the box.

SPELLING LIST

bow
bowl
crow
own
show
slow
boat
coach
goal
goat
road
soap

coach   bow   goat   crow   boat   bowl

oa	ow

Blank Out

Fill in the missing "oa" or "ow" in these sentences.

1. Let me sh__ __ you how to do that.

2. Greg was going too sl__ __, so I gave him a push.

3. Ayla poured cereal into her b__ __l.

4. TJ scored the winning g__ __l at the soccer game.

5. Mike doesn't __ __n any fancy clothes.

6. The c__ __ch showed me a better way to kick the ball.

7. I hold my father's hand when I cross the r__ __d.

8. I couldn't find any s__ __p for my bath.

The Long "O" Show

Knock Out

CROSS OUT the pictures that show words that **don't** have a long **o** sound.

WRITE the words for the pictures you didn't cross out.

_____   _____

_____   _____

Word Scramble

UNSCRAMBLE each word and write it correctly. LOOK at the word box for help. CROSS OUT each word in the word box as you make it.

| bow | crow | own | show | slow | boat | coach | goal | goat | road |

1. atob _____

2. rdoa _____

3. wob _____

4. wrco _____

5. algo _____

6. accoh _____

7. onw _____

8. oatg _____

9. oslw _____

10. swho _____

The New, True Long "U"

Blank Out

FILL IN the missing "ue," "ui," "oo," or "ew" in these sentences.

1. Grab a **br_____m** and sweep up.

2. I still have a **f_____** things to do before we go.

3. Mom always tells me to **ch_____** my food before I swallow.

4. None of the things Billy told me about Mars were **tr_____**.

5. Tony **thr_____** the ball to Jamal.

6. I like to have **fr_____t** in my cereal.

7. The sun shone down on the **bl_____** sea.

8. Andrea plans to be the first woman on the **m_____n**.

Knock Out

CROSS OUT the pictures that show words that **don't** have a long **u** sound.

WRITE the words for the pictures you didn't cross out.

_____   _____

_____   _____

Word Blocks

FILL IN the word blocks with words of the same shape from the word box. Use the pictures as clues.

| blue | glue | boot | broom | tooth | fruit |

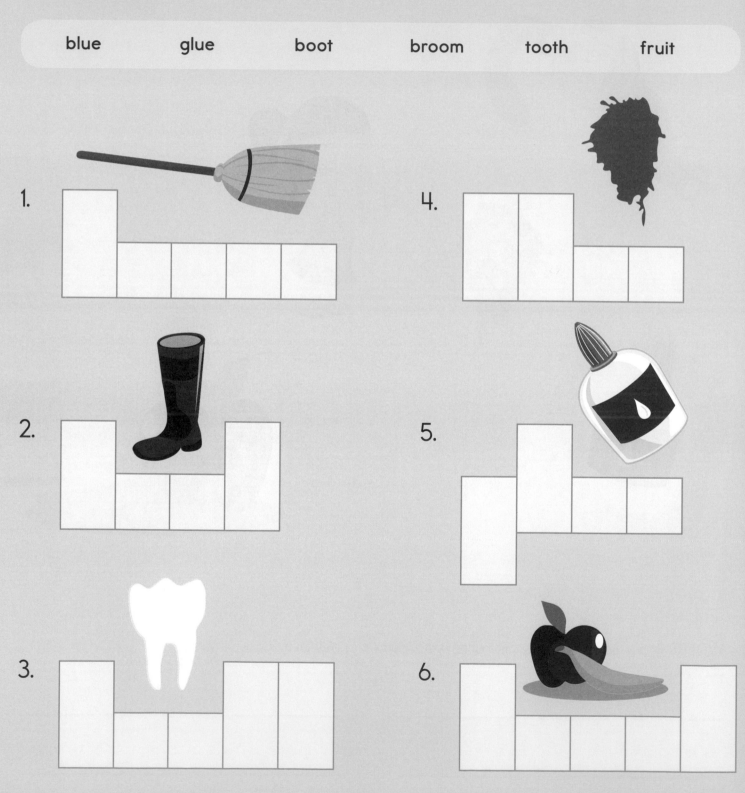

1.

2.

3.

4.

5.

6.

Word Scramble

UNSCRAMBLE each word and write it correctly. LOOK at the word box for help.
CROSS OUT each word in the word box as you make it.

| glue | true | few | chew | threw | flew | boot | broom | moon | tooth |

1. rewht _____

2. efw _____

3. hcwe _____

4. welf _____

5. noom _____

6. rteu _____

7. elgu _____

8. ottho _____

9. rmboo _____

10. oobt _____

You Old Soft "C"!

Sort and Spell

The letter "c" can make a hard **k** sound, as in *cook*, or soft **s** sound, as in *twice*. LISTEN for the soft or hard **c** in each word pictured. DRAW a line from the picture to the correct sound box. WRITE the word in the box.

SPELLING LIST

face

race

place

space

trace

ice

mice

nice

price

slice

twice

city

cake

clock

Soft **c**

Hard **c**

Blank Out

FILL TN the missing "ace" or "ice" to complete words with the soft c sound.

1. One way to learn how to draw is to **tr**_____

   other pictures.

2. Wipe that smile off your **f**_____, Mister!

3. It was Cale's party, so he had a second **sl**_____

   of cake.

4. It was very **n**_____ of you to give me your seat.

5. Someday Bess is going to fly a rocket into **sp**_____.

6. I won't buy this. The **pr**_____ is too high.

7. Fido couldn't find a good **pl**_____ to bury his bone.

8. The cheese goes so fast in our house, Mom says

   we must have **m**_____.

9. I'll **r**_____ you home!

10. That movie was so good, we watched it **tw**_____.

Match Up

The letter "g" can make both a hard **g** sound, as in *gum,* or a soft **j** sound, as in *age.* WRITE the word from the word box that matches each picture. CIRCLE the pictures that show words that make the **j** sound.

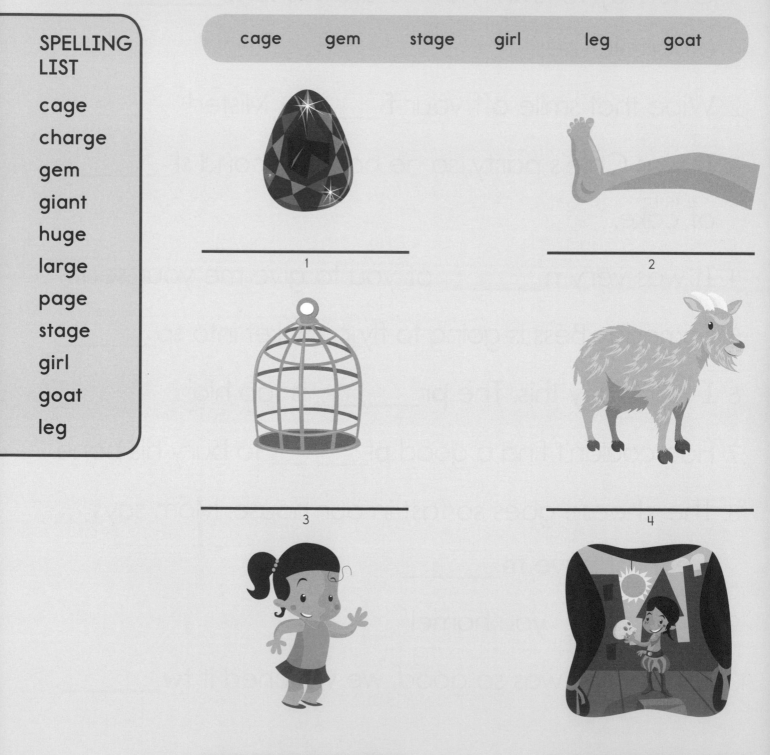

SPELLING
LIST

cage
charge
gem
giant
huge
large
page
stage
girl
goat
leg

cage   gem   stage   girl   leg   goat

1

2

3

4

5

6

Word Scramble

UNSCRAMBLE each word and write it correctly. LOOK at the word box for help.
CROSS OUT each word in the word box as you make it.

cage	charge	gem	giant	huge	large	page	stage

1. meg _____

2. aglre _____

3. ghue _____

4. hregac _____

5. gesat _____

6. intga _____

7. geap _____

8. geca _____

UNSCRAMBLE the words to complete the riddle.

Q. Why did the monster buy a **igtan** battery?

_____

A. He needed a **lrgae hgaerc.**

_____ _____

Blank Out

FILL IN the missing word to complete the sentence.

SPELLING LIST

could

might

should

would

1. I **sh**_____ keep looking at these words if I want to learn them.

2. Kayla said she **w**_____ try the spinach.

3. **W**_____ you keep an eye on Scamp?

4. I **m**_____ make it home if the bus ever comes.

5. Jamal **c**_____ do even the hardest math.

6. You **sh**_____ never be afraid to ask.

7. I **c**_____ sure use a hot fudge sundae right now.

Word Hunt

CIRCLE the words from the word box in the grid. Words go across and down, not diagonally or backward. Each word appears twice!

might	could	should	would

```
s h o u l d i o
r i c o u l d u
m w u d c s h l
i o m i g h t d
g u o u c o u l
h l l c o u l d
t d w o u l d a
l i g h t d o u
```

WRITE each word that you circled.

_____   _____

_____   _____

The Edge of "J"

Blank Out

FILL IN the missing "j" or "dge" to complete the sentence.

SPELLING
LIST

bridge

dodge

edge

fudge

hedge

judge

lodge

ridge

jelly

juice

joke

1. Maya loves to eat _____**elly** beans.

2. Deshi is really good at **do**_____ ball.

3. I think a troll lives under this **bri**_____.

4. Lin has a glass of _____**uice**

   every morning.

5. The scouts had a meeting at the **lo**_____.

6. Mom makes the best **fu**_____ in the world!

7. Max really knows how to tell a _____**oke**.

8. I get scared when I stand too close to

   the **e**_____.

Write and Rhyme

FILL IN the word from the Spelling List that best fits the picture. Then WRITE another word from the list that rhymes with it.

1

_____

_____

2

_____

_____

3

_____

_____

4

_____

_____

Word Scramble

UNSCRAMBLE each word and write it correctly. Look at the Spelling List for help.

SPELLING LIST

curve
serve
swerve
have
move
prove
dove
glove
love
shove
give
live

1. vepro _____

2. emvo _____

3. lvoeg _____

4. vlei _____

5. ovseh _____

6. aevh _____

7. elov _____

8. eivg _____

9. rseve _____

10. odev _____

11. wreves _____

12. cruve _____

Blank Out!

FILL IN the word from the Spelling List that best fits the sentence.

1. Tasha has a mean _____ at Ping-Pong!

2. Please don't _____! We'll all make it onto the bus.

3. This is the house where I _____.

4. During the quake, Dan could feel the earth _____.

5. The car had to _____ so it wouldn't hit the deer.

6. Would you _____ me a hand with this?

7. The sign warned us of a _____ in the road.

8. I think I'll _____ a triple-fudge sundae for dessert.

9. _____, _____, and _____ all rhyme with shove, and I can _____ it!

Silent as a Lamb

Who's Hiding?

LOOK at the word box. CIRCLE the silent letter or letters in each word.
WRITE each word in the box labeled with the silent letter.

caught	daughter	thumb	knife	lamb	walk
talk	knee	wrong	comb	sign	write

SPELLING LIST

caught

daughter

thumb

comb

lamb

walk

talk

knee

knife

wrong

write

sign

b

g

k

l

w

Not Quite!

CIRCLE the words that are misspelled in this story.

The king said to his dotter, "Your hair is a mess. You need to cowm it."

"Rong!" she said. "Tock to the hand!" But she cot her thum in her hair. "This is a bad sayn," she said. She tried to pull free, but soon her hands and her feet were stuck in her hair. She couldn't even wok.

"That's it," said the king. He got a nife and cut her hair short. Now she doesn't need a comb!

WRITE the circled words correctly.

_____   _____

_____   _____

_____   _____

_____

Commonly Misspelled Words

There Their!

There is about a place, and *their* is about people. For example, *Their key was there.*
WRITE the right form of *there* or *their* to complete each sentence.

SPELLING
LIST

again

because

favorite

friend

people

said

they

there

their

were

_____ were once three little pigs. _____
1   2

mother sent them out into the world.

"Hold on!" said one pig. "_____ are wolves
                                                    3

out here!" So they put _____ heads
                                              4

together, and decided to get a house.

"_____ is a nice house," said one pig,
        5

pointing to a straw house. "You're kidding,

right?" said the others. That was _____ first
                                                                6

fight. In the middle of _____ argument, a wolf
                                          7

came by. "_____ is nothing like brick to keep wolves
                    8

out," he said. He sold them a nice brick house.

"Wait," said the pigs. "Why didn't you eat us?"

"_____ is more money in real estate," said the wolf.
        9

He bought a nice steak dinner.

Word Hunt

CIRCLE the words from the word box in the grid. Words go across and down, not diagonally or backward.

because	they	people	favorite	friend	were	said	again

```
t  b  r  a  g  a  i  n
h  e  n  d  a  f  r  t
e  c  a  w  e  r  e  h
f  a  v  o  r  i  t  e
s  u  d  r  a  e  p  y
a  s  a  i  n  n  d  a
i  e  o  p  l  d  g  h
d  a  p  e  o  p  l  e
```

WRITE each word that you circled.

_____   _____

_____   _____

_____   _____

_____   _____

Commonly Misspelled Words

Blank Out

WRITE the word from the word box that best fits the sentence.

~~because~~ ~~they~~ ~~people~~ ~~favorite~~ ~~friend~~ ~~Were~~ ~~said~~ ~~again~~

1. Carlos likes to skate with his __friend__ Kiki.

2. Some __people__ are born lucky.

3. My stomach hurt __because__ I ate too much.

4. I didn't hear you. Could you tell me that __again__?

5. Eddie and Ming bought everything __they__ saw.

6. Jake's mother __said__ he was late.

7. __Were__ you able to answer that last question?

8. No one believes that snails are my __favorite__ food.

176

Word Scramble

UNSCRAMBLE each word and write it correctly. LOOK at the word box for help.
CROSS OUT each word in the word box as you make it.

~~because~~ ~~there~~	~~they~~ ~~friend~~	~~people~~ ~~were~~	~~favorite~~ ~~said~~	their ~~again~~

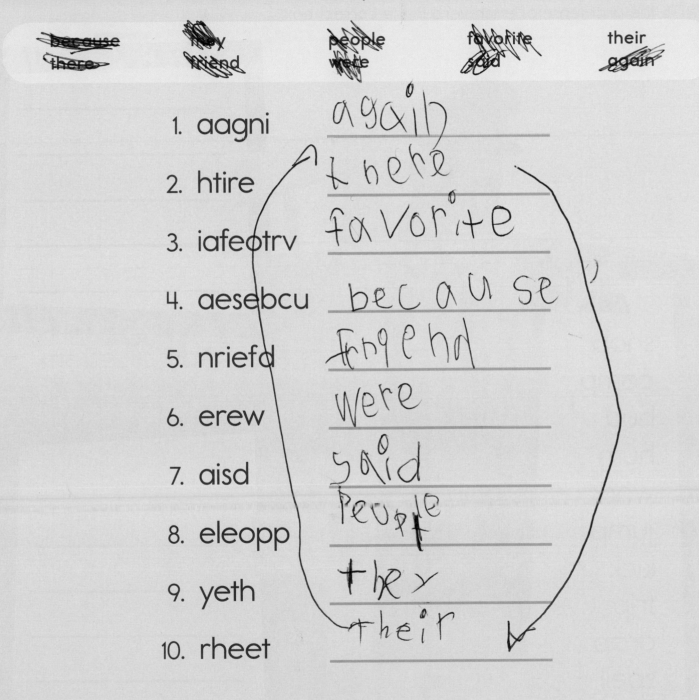

1. aagni   again

2. htire   there

3. iafeotrv   favorite

4. aesebcu   because

5. nriefd   frnehd

6. erew   were

7. aisd   said

8. eleopp   people

9. yeth   they

10. rheet   their

Double or Nothing!

To make a verb past tense, you usually add "-ed." When the verb has a short vowel and ends with one consonant, you usually double the consonant first. WRITE the past tense of each verb in the correct box.

shop
camp
hug
hum
work
jump
kick
trip
drop
spell

Add a Letter

Ready to Go

Make Room!

Usually when a verb ends in "e," you remove the final "e" before adding "ed" to the word. WRITE the past tense of each verb in the correct box.

poke
mark
look
dine
learn
bake
rake
joke
chew
glow

Remove the **e**

Ready to Go

Sort and Spell

READ each word and listen to how it sounds. In some words, the "d" at the end makes a **d** sound. In others, it makes a **t** sound.

MARK each word with a T or a D. Then WRITE the word in the correct word box.

○ hugged

○ seemed

○ kicked

○ tripped

○ served

○ climbed

○ baked

○ jumped

○ piled

○ camped

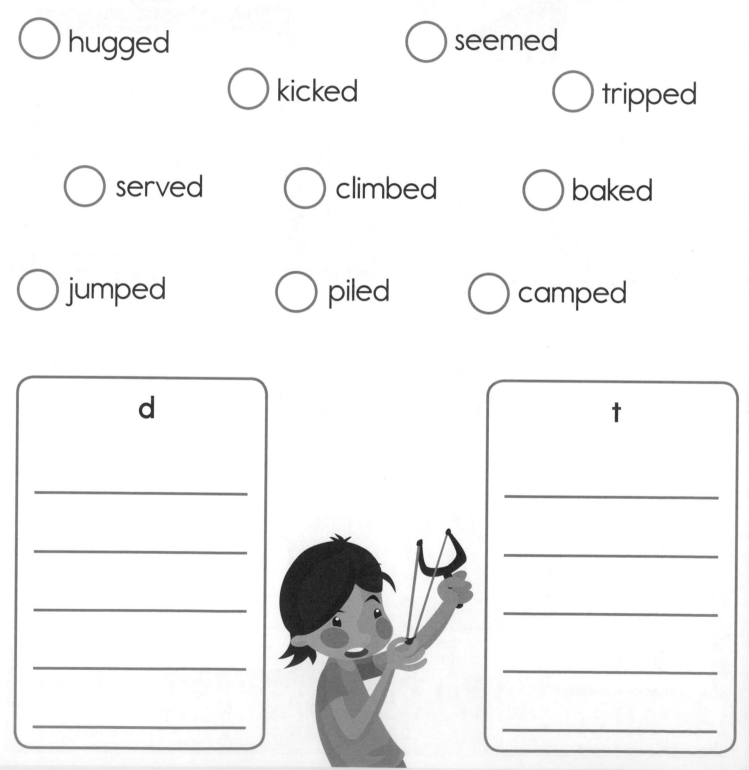

d	**t**
_____	_____
_____	_____
_____	_____
_____	_____

Extra Baggage

CIRCLE the words in which the "-ed" adds an extra syllable to the word.
WRITE the words in the correct boxes.

joked

shouted

marked

grinned

tasted

chewed

sipped

darted

rested

nodded

No Extra Baggage

_____

_____

_____

_____

_____

Extra Baggage

_____

_____

_____

_____

The "-Ing" Thing

Samurai Speller!

CROSS OUT the final "e" in the words below.
WRITE the correct form of the word with
"-ing" at the end.

dive + ing = diving

1. bake   + ing   = _____

2. pile   + ing   = _____

3. joke   + ing   = _____

4. serve   + ing   = _____

5. live   + ing   = _____

6. poke   + ing   = _____

7. dine   + ing   = _____

8. taste   + ing   = _____

9. prove   + ing   = _____

10. rake   + ing   = _____

Double Up

ADD a second consonant to the end of each word. WRITE the correct form of the word with "-ing" on the end.

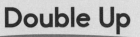

nod + d + ing = nodding

1. rub   + ___ + ing = _____

2. dip   + ___ + ing = _____

3. drop + ___ + ing = _____

4. plan + ___ + ing = _____

5. hum   + ___ + ing = _____

6. shop + ___ + ing = _____

7. trip   + ___ + ing = _____

8. grin   + ___ + ing = _____

9. plan   + ___ + ing = _____

10. chat + ___ + ing = _____

The "-Ing" Thing

This Way Please!

WRITE the "-ing" form of each word in the correct box. CROSS OUT each word as you write it.

shop

taste

dive

hug

mark

serve

camp

lock

drop

joke

bake

plan

sip

gulp

kick

Double Final Consonant

_____

_____

_____

_____

_____

Drop Final **e**

_____

_____

_____

_____

_____

Leave Alone

_____

_____

_____

_____

_____

Two's Company

WRITE the plural form of each word by adding "-s" to the end.

1. pig   + _____ = _____

2. cape   + _____ = _____

3. path   + _____ = _____

4. belt   + _____ = _____

5. stick + _____ = _____

6. truck + _____ = _____

7. king   + _____ = _____

8. lamp   + _____ = _____

9. nest   + _____ = _____

10. carrot + _____ = _____

To "E" or Not to "E"

ADD an "-es" to these words to make them plural.

1. glass   + _____   = _____

2. witch   + _____   = _____

3. dish   + _____   = _____

4. fox   + _____   = _____

5. lash   + _____   = _____

6. wish   + _____   = _____

7. guess   + _____   = _____

8. bus   + _____   = _____

9. miss   + _____   = _____

10. box   + _____   = _____

11. watch   + _____   = _____

12. itch   + _____   = _____

"S" Is More

Sort and Spell

LISTEN for the sound the "s" makes at the end of each word. DRAW a line from the picture to the correct sound box. WRITE the word in the box.

bananas   books   chairs   girls   sticks   trucks

S	Z

Extra Baggage

CIRCLE the words where the "s" or "es" adds an extra syllable to the word.
WRITE the words in the correct boxes.

glasses

witches

itches

cards

baths

showers

boots

carrots

buses

matches

No Extra Baggage

_____

_____

_____

_____

_____

Extra Baggage

_____

_____

_____

_____

_____

Odd Men Out

Word Scramble

Some words form plurals in unusual ways:

End in EN	OO → EE	OUSE → ICE	No Change
man → men woman → women child → children	foot → feet tooth → teeth	mouse → mice	sheep deer fish

UNSCRAMBLE each word and write it correctly. LOOK at the word box for help.

1. ftee _____

2. meonw _____

3. tehet _____

4. cmie _____

5. delicrnh _____

Word Hunt

CIRCLE the plural words from the word box in the grid. Words go across and down, not diagonally or backward.

| men | women | children | feet | teeth | mice | deer | sheep | fish |

f	i	m	w	o	m	e	n
m	o	u	n	e	g	t	w
i	c	f	e	e	t	e	o
c	h	i	l	d	r	e	n
e	o	s	f	e	w	t	d
e	s	h	e	e	p	h	r
m	e	n	e	r	e	n	e

WRITE each word that you circled.

_____   _____

_____   _____

_____   _____

Blank Out

FILL IN the missing "-er" or "-est" in these sentences.

1. Chip is pretty tall, but Jason is

   tall_____.

2. King Midas must have been the

   rich_____ person in the world!

3. I wish this knife were **sharp**_____. I can't cut

   anything with it.

4. This is the **soft**_____ pillow I've ever had.

5. Mom was proud of me for winning the game, but

   even **proud**_____ for being a good sport.

6. If this hill gets any **steep**_____, I won't be able to get

   to the top.

7. Lola thought she had the **kind**_____ grandmother

   ever!

So Lonesome...

When a word has a short vowel sound and ends with one consonant, double that consonant before adding "-er" or "-est."

DOUBLE the last consonant. WRITE the correct form of each word.

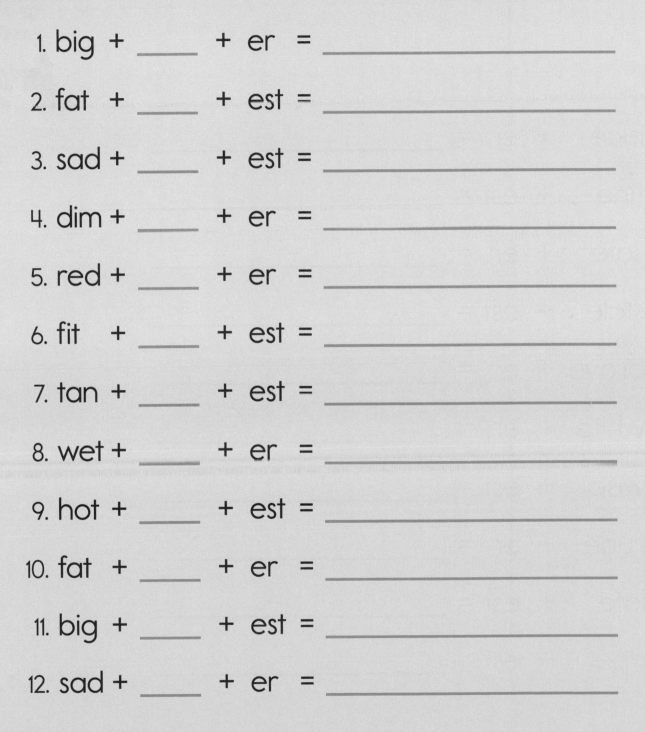

1. big + _____ + er = _____

2. fat + _____ + est = _____

3. sad + _____ + est = _____

4. dim + _____ + er = _____

5. red + _____ + er = _____

6. fit + _____ + est = _____

7. tan + _____ + est = _____

8. wet + _____ + er = _____

9. hot + _____ + est = _____

10. fat + _____ + er = _____

11. big + _____ + est = _____

12. sad + _____ + er = _____

Samurai Speller!

CROSS OUT the final "e" in the words. WRITE the correct form of the word with "-er" or "-est" at the end.

1. nice   + er = _____

2. fine   + est = _____

3. safe   + er = _____

4. stale   + est = _____

5. brave   + er = _____

6. white   + er = _____

7. wise   + est = _____

8. rude   + er = _____

9. late   + est = _____

10. ripe   + est = _____

Not Quite!

CIRCLE the words that are misspelled in this story.

The bigest mistake I made was staying latter than I should have. The sky was getting darkker. The wind was blowing the wilddest I had ever seen. Mom, who's oldder and wisser than I am, said I should hurry home. "I'm not scared," I said. "I'm braveer than that."

Brave, maybe, but not the smarttest.

It rained hardder than ever. When I got home, I was weter than I'd ever been.

WRITE the circled words correctly.

1. _____

2. _____

3. _____

4. _____

5. _____

6. _____

7. _____

8. _____

9. _____

10. _____

"-Er" and "-Est"

Quick Change

CROSS OUT the final "y" in each word and change it to an "i." Then WRITE the correct form of the word with "-er" or "-est."

1. dry   + _____ + er = _____

2. lovely   + _____ + est = _____

3. pretty   + _____ + est = _____

4. skinny   + _____ + er = _____

5. noisy   + _____ + er = _____

6. funny   + _____ + est = _____

7. ugly   + _____ + est = _____

8. heavy   + _____ + er = _____

9. lucky   + _____ + est = _____

10. early   + _____ + er = _____

11. sandy   + _____ + est = _____

12. friendly   + _____ + er = _____

Word Hunt

CIRCLE the words from the word box in the grid. Words go across and down, not diagonally or backward.

driest   earlier   funniest   goofiest   heaviest   meatier   prettier   tastier

e	r	o	g	o	o	f	i	e	s	t
a	e	s	t	p	r	e	d	i	e	a
r	o	o	f	y	d	o	r	b	d	s
l	e	a	f	u	n	n	i	e	s	t
i	p	r	e	t	t	i	e	r	s	i
e	h	e	a	v	i	e	s	t	i	e
r	f	u	n	m	e	a	t	i	e	r

WRITE each word that you circled.

_____   _____

_____   _____

_____   _____

Review

This Way Please!

WRITE the "-er" form of each word in the correct box. CROSS OUT each word as you write it.

skinny

dry

wet

heavy

ripe

big

brave

nice

noisy

wise

sad

funny

fine

fat

hot

Double Final Consonant

_____

_____

_____

_____

_____

Drop Final **e**

_____

_____

_____

_____

_____

Change **y** to **i**

_____

_____

_____

_____

_____

Word Scramble

UNSCRAMBLE each word and write it correctly. LOOK at the word box for help. CROSS OUT each word in the word box as you make it.

bravest	older	loveliest	strangest	smaller	richest
skinniest	clearest	cleaner	bigger	stronger	wiser

1. agrstenst _____

2. bgeigr _____

3. grersnot _____

4. arnlece _____

5. slelrma _____

6. eeilvtlso _____

7. aeseltcr _____

8. elrdo _____

9. sitskneni _____

10. streich _____

11. avsebtr _____

12. sweri _____

Page 108
1. big bug
2. hot hat
3. bad bed
4. nut net
5. hip hop

Page 109
ACROSS   DOWN
1. cat   2. top
3. mop   4. pup
6. pet   5. hit
8. pit   7. tub
10. tag   9. ten
11. bed

Page 110
1. hope, hop
2. made, mad
3. pet, Pete
4. cute, cut
5. fine, fin

Page 111
1. cut → cute
2. gav → gave
3. pok → poke
4. mad → made
5. hid → hide
6. hat → hate
7. hop → hope
8. tim → time

Page 112
1. white
2. chop
3. thick
4. shop
5. chat
6. ship
7. thin
8. when

Page 113
1. chick
2. white
3. shapes
4. ship
5. chop
6. shop

Page 114
1. ship
2. thin
3. what
4. chick
5. white
6. chop
7. chat
8. shapes
9. thick
10. shop

Page 115
1. thick, thin
2. chick chat
3. ship shape

Page 116
1. fish
2. with
3. which
4. watch
5. dash
6. math
7. witch
8. catch

Page 117
1. bath
2. rich
3. catch
4. dash

Page 118
1. math
2. rich
3. watch
4. bath
5. fish
6. witch

Page 119
1. whish → which
2. wich → witch
3. ritsh → rich
4. catsh → catch
5. fich → fish
6. maf → math
7. wif → with
8. datsh → dash

Page 120
1. dress
2. skirt
3. shirt
4. coat
5. shoe
6. belt
7. shorts
8. pants

Page 121

Page 122
Cross out: duck, kite
Write: truck, frog, stick, slide

Page 123
1. clam
2. spill
3. trap
4. frog
5. steps
6. crab

Page 124
1. truck
2. frog
3. stick
4. trap
5. slip
6. crab
7. slide
8. trip

Page 125
1. slip
2. trap
3. steps
4. clam
5. stick
6. crab
7. stop
8. spill
9. slide
10. trip
11. frog
12. truck

Pages 126–127
1. hand
2. desk
3. lamp
4. gift
5. nest
6. mask
7. jump
8. tent
9. cast
10. ant
11. camp
12. band

Page 128
1. capm → camp
2. tenk → tent
3. ankt → ant
4. hamd → hand
5. ness → nest
6. jum → jump
7. casp → cast

Page 129
Cross out: fan, clam, key
Write: desk, lamp, gift, mask

Page 130
1. pizza
2. milk
3. carrot
4. banana
5. bread
6. cookie
7. steak
8. apple

Page 131

Page 132
1. part
2. chirp
3. skirt
4. hurt
5. first
6. bird
7. chart

Page 133
girl: her, chirp, first, hurt, turn, bird, skirt, worm
car: card, chart, hard, part

Page 134
1. card
2. chart
3. hard
4. bird
5. worm
6. first
7. turn
8. hurt
9. skirt
10. part
11. chirp
12. her

Page 135
1. hord → hard
2. ferst → first
3. heer → her
4. port → part
5. hert → hurt
6. torn → turn
7. berd → bird
8. werm → worm

Page 136
1. deer
2. store
3. gear
4. chair

Page 137
Dear, deer

1. gear
2. cheer
3. steer
4. dear
5. near

Page 138
1. share
2. care
3. store
4. pair
5. dare
6. chair
7. more
8. hair

Page 139
1. pair
2. cheer
3. gear
4. near
5. chair
6. steer
7. more
8. dare
9. share
10. store

Answers

Page 140

```
w  e  a  t  c (w  e  r
a  o  u  d (r  a  i  n)
r  a  w  e  i  r  s  c
(s  h  o  c  n  m  h) l
n (c  l  o  u  d) o  o
o  n  d  l  i  n  w  u
(w  i  n  d) d  w  e  r
(w  e  a  t  h  e  r) m
```

Page 141
1. rain
2. warm
3. cold
4. wind
5. weather
6. cloud
7. shower
8. snow

Page 142
ay: gray, play, tray
ai: paint, train, snail

Page 143
Cross out: car, gear
Write: weight, mail, braid, snail

Page 144
1. mail
2. weigh
3. train
4. paint
5. say
6. play
7. neighbor
8. gray

Page 145
1. plai → play
2. nayber → neighbor
3. mayl → mail
4. gra → gray
5. brade → braid
6. wey → weigh
7. snale → snail
8. sae → say

Page 146
ea: beach, leaf, seal
ee: green, teeth, wheel

Page 147
1. candy, puppy, teeth
2. monkey, tree, speak

Page 148
Cross out: worm, yo-yo
Write: key, candy, tree, puppy

Page 149
1. wheel
2. beach
3. seal
4. teeth
5. monkey
6. green
7. key
8. puppy
9. leaf
10. speak

Page 150
1. kind
2. blind
3. try
4. sigh
5. high
6. find
7. light
8. bright

Page 151
1. bright light
2. right mind
3. fly spy

Page 152

```
s (f  l  y) i  t  e
(b  r  i  g  h  t) n
(h) i  g  i  n  r  d
i  f  h  y  k  y  g
g  t  t  g  i  h  s
(h) b  l  i  n  d) p
s (m  i  n  d) i  o
```

Page 153
1. kind
2. find
3. mind
4. high
5. blind
6. bright
7. spy
8. right
9. light
10. sigh

Page 154
oa: boat, coach, goat
ow: bow, bowl, crow

Page 155
1. show
2. slow
3. bowl
4. goal
5. own
6. coach
7. road
8. soap

Page 156
Cross out: gear, fork
Write: goal, soap, road, bowl

Page 157
1. boat
2. road
3. bow
4. crow
5. goal
6. coach
7. own
8. goat
9. slow
10. show

Page 158
1. broom
2. few
3. chew
4. true
5. threw
6. fruit
7. blue
8. moon

Page 159
Cross out: watch, girl
Write: blue, moon, glue, fruit

Page 160
1. broom
2. boot
3. tooth
4. blue
5. glue
6. fruit

Page 161
1. threw
2. few
3. chew
4. flew
5. moon
6. true
7. glue
8. tooth
9. broom
10. boot

Page 162
Soft c: face, ice, city, mice
Hard c: clock, cake

Page 163
1. trace
2. face
3. slice
4. nice
5. space
6. price
7. place
8. mice
9. race
10. twice

Page 164
1. gem
2. leg
3. cage
4. goat
5. girl
6. stage
Circle: gem, cage, stage

Page 165
1. gem
2. large
3. huge
4. charge
5. stage
6. giant
7. page
8. cage

Riddle: giant, large charge

Page 166
1. should
2. would
3. Would
4. might
5. could
6. should
7. could

Page 167

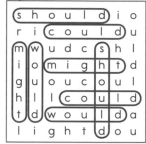

```
(s  h  o  u  l  d) i  o
r  i (c  o  u  l  d) u
(m)(w  u  d  c  s  h) l
i  o  o (m  i  g  h  t) d
g  u  o  u  c  o  u  l
h  l  l (c  o  u  l  d)
t (w  o  u  l  d) a
l  i  g  h  t) d  o  u
```

Page 168
1. jelly
2. dodge
3. bridge
4. juice
5. lodge
6. fudge
7. joke
8. edge

Page 169
1. judge, fudge
2. bridge, ridge
3. lodge, dodge
4. hedge, edge

Page 170
1. prove
2. move
3. glove
4. live
5. shove
6. have
7. love
8. give
9. serve
10. dove
11. swerve
12. curve

Page 171
1. serve
2. shove
3. live
4. move
5. swerve
6. give
7. curve
8. have
9. Dove, glove, love, prove

Page 172
b: comb, thumb, lamb
g: caught, daughter, sign
k: knee, knife
l: walk, talk
w: wrong, write

Page 173
1. dotter → daughter
2. cowm → comb
3. rong → wrong
4. tock → talk
5. cot → caught
6. thum → thumb
7. sayn → sign
8. wok → walk
9. nife → knife

Page 174
1. There
2. Their
3. There
4. their
5. There
6. their
7. their
8. There
9. There

Page 175

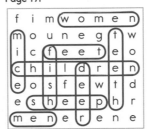

Page 176
1. friend
2. people
3. because
4. again
5. they
6. said
7. Were
8. favorite

Page 177
1. again
2. their
3. favorite
4. because
5. friend
6. were
7. said
8. people
9. they
10. there

Page 178
Add a Letter: shopped, hugged, hummed, tripped, dropped
Ready to Go: camped, worked, jumped, kicked, spelled

Page 179
Remove the e: poked, dined, baked, raked, joked
Ready to Go: marked, looked, learned, chewed, glowed

Page 180
d: served, piled, seemed, climbed, hugged
t: kicked, jumped, tripped, camped, baked

Page 181
No extra baggage: joked, chewed, sipped, grinned, marked
Extra baggage (circled): shouted, darted, rested, tasted, nodded

Page 182
1. baking
2. piling
3. joking
4. serving
5. living
6. poking
7. dining
8. tasting
9. proving
10. raking

Page 183
1. b, rubbing
2. p, dipping
3. p, dropping
4. n, planning
5. m, humming
6. p, shopping
7. p, tripping
8. n, grinning
9. n, planning
10. t, chatting

Pages 184–185
Drop Final e: diving, tasting, serving, joking, baking
Double Final Consonant: shopping, hugging, sipping, dropping, planning
Leave Alone: gulping, locking, camping, marking, kicking

Page 186
1. s, pigs
2. s, capes
3. s, paths
4. s, belts
5. s, sticks
6. s, trucks
7. s, kings
8. s, lamps
9. s, nests
10. s, carrots

Page 187
1. es, glasses
2. es, witches
3. es, dishes
4. es, foxes
5. es, lashes
6. es, wishes
7. es, guesses
8. es, buses
9. es, misses
10. es, boxes
11. es, watches
12. es, itches

Page 188
s: books, sticks, trucks
z: bananas, girls, chairs

Page 189
Extra baggage (circled): glasses, witches, itches, matches, buses
No extra baggage: cards, showers, boots, baths, carrots

Page 190
1. feet
2. women
3. teeth
4. mice
5. children

Page 191

```
f i m (w o m e n)
(m) o u n e g t  w
 i c (f e e t) e  o
(c h i l d r e n)
 e o s f e w t d
 e (s h e e p) h  r
(m e n) e r e n e
```

Page 192
1. taller
2. richest
3. sharper
4. softest
5. prouder
6. steeper
7. kindest

Page 193
1. g, bigger
2. t, fattest
3. d, saddest
4. m, dimmer
5. d, redder
6. t, fittest
7. n, tannest
8. t, wetter
9. t, hottest
10. t, fatter
11. g, biggest
12. d, sadder

Page 194
1. nicer
2. finest
3. safer
4. stalest
5. braver
6. whiter
7. wisest
8. ruder
9. latest
10. ripest

Page 195
1. bigest → biggest
2. latter → later
3. darkker → darker
4. wilddest → wildest
5. oldder → older
6. wisser → wiser
7. braver → braver
8. smartest → smartest
9. hardder → harder
10. weter → wetter

Page 196
1. i, drier
2. i, loveliest
3. i, prettiest
4. i, skinnier
5. i, noisier
6. i, funniest
7. i, ugliest
8. i, heavier
9. i, luckiest
10. i, earlier
11. i, sandiest
12. i, friendlier

Page 197

```
(e r o (g o o f i e s t)
 a e s t p r e d i e a
 r o o f y d o r b d s
 l e a (f u n n i e s t)
(i (p r e t t i e r) s i
 e (h e a v i e s t i e
 r f u n (m e a t i e r)
```

Pages 198–199
Drop Final e: finer, wiser, braver, riper, nicer
Double Final Consonant: fatter, wetter, hotter, sadder, bigger
Change y to i: skinnier, funnier, heavier, drier, noisier

Page 200
1. strangest
2. bigger
3. stronger
4. cleaner
5. smaller
6. loveliest
7. clearest
8. older
9. skinniest
10. richest
11. bravest
12. wiser

2nd Grade
Vocabulary Puzzles

Look It Up

Word List

READ the words and their meanings.

ad·jec·tive—AJ-ihk-tihv *noun* a word that describes something, like *pretty* or *blue*

def·i·ni·tion—dehf-uh-NIHSH-uhn *noun* the meaning of a word

de·scribe—dih-SKRIB *verb* to make a picture with words, like "a pretty girl in a blue dress"

dic·tion·ar·y—DIHK-shuh-nehr-ee *noun* a book filled with definitions of words

mean·ing—MEE-nihng *noun* the idea of a word, what it means

noun—nown *noun* a word that stands for a person, place, or thing

verb—verb *noun* a word that stands for an action, like *run*

Match the Meaning

WRITE the words next to their definitions. LOOK at the word box for help.

adjective	definition	dictionary	meaning
noun	~~describe~~	verb	

1. **describe**   to make a word picture

2. _____ the idea of a word

3. _____ an action word

4. _____ a word for a person, place, or thing

5. _____ a word that describes something

6. _____ a book filled with definitions

7. _____ the meaning of a word

ABC-123

Words in a dictionary go in **alphabetical order**. That means words that start with "A" go before words that start with "B."

READ the words in the word box. Then WRITE them in alphabetical order.

| machine | octopus | jelly | whisper |
| balloon | trouble | ~~angry~~ | learn |

1. __angry__

2. _____

3. _____

4. _____

5. _____

6. _____

7. _____

8. _____

A B C D E F G H I J K L M N O P Q R S T U V W X Y Z

Pick the One

A **dictionary** tells you whether a word is a *noun, adjective,* or *verb.*
Those are **parts of speech.**

CIRCLE the correct part of speech for each word.

HINT: If you're not sure, look up the words in a dictionary.

1. **eat**   noun   adjective   (verb)

2. **purple**   noun   adjective   verb

3. **draw**   noun   adjective   verb

4. **animal**   noun   adjective   verb

5. **young**   noun   adjective   verb

6. **wash**   noun   adjective   verb

7. **tooth**   noun   adjective   verb

8. **stove**   noun   adjective   verb

Look It Up

Dictionary Dare

Guide words are the first and last words on a page in a dictionary. They help you figure out if the word you're looking for is on that page.

READ the guide words. CIRCLE the word in each row that comes between them.

HINT: The words are in alphabetical order. Use the second letter of each word to figure out which word should come in between.

1. **folk → football**   (food)   frost   find

2. **preschool → president**   peace   puppy   present

3. **trade → train**   tuck   taxi   traffic

4. **robot → roller coaster** recess   rock   rumble

5. **babble → balloon**   bagpipes   beaver   blob

6. **mold → money**   missile   monarch   mucus

7. **uniform → unlucky**   umpire   useless   unique

8. **haunt → hazy**   hawk   hero   hungry

480   **folk • football**

folk \fōk\ *n. pl* **folk** or **folks**
1 *archaic*: a group of kindr
: PEOPLE **2** : the great p
determines the g
characteristic f

Blank Out

A dictionary also tells you how many syllables a word has. A **syllable** is each part of a word that takes one beat to say. So *mean* has one syllable and *meaning* has two syllables. A dot shows the break for each syllable: *mean·ing*.

READ each word out loud. Then WRITE the number of syllables.

1. ad·jec·tive   3

2. def·i·ni·tion

3. de·scribe

4. dic·tion·ar·y

5. mean·ing

6. noun

7. syl·la·ble

8. verb

Same and Opposite

Word List

READ the words and their meanings.

ar·rive—uh-RIV *verb* to come to a place

at·tempt—uh-TEHMPT *verb* to try to do something

beau·ti·ful—BYOO-tuh-fuhl *adjective* very pretty

en·e·my—EHN-uh-mee *noun* someone who is working against you, a foe

fail—fayl *verb* to lose, to not get what you tried for

gi·ant—JI-uhnt 1. *noun* a huge person or other creature out of a fairy tale 2. *adjective* very big

pred·a·tor—PREHD-uh-ter *noun* an animal or insect that hunts others for its food

suc·ceed—suhk-SEED *verb* to win, to get what you wanted

Match the Meaning

WRITE the words next to their definitions. LOOK at the word box for help.

arrive	attempt	beautiful	enemy
fail	giant	predator	succeed

1. _____ really large

2. _____ to lose

3. _____ to win

4. _____ a hunter

5. _____ to come

6. _____ really pretty

7. _____ to try

8. _____ someone who's out to get you

Same and Opposite

Pick the One

Some words mean the same thing, like *start* and *begin*. Others are **opposites**, like *night* and *day*.

READ each word pair. CIRCLE "same" if they have the same meaning and "opposite" if the words are opposites.

1. **arrive**	**leave**	same	opposite
2. **giant**	**huge**	same	opposite
3. **fail**	**succeed**	same	opposite
4. **beautiful**	**ugly**	same	opposite
5. **attempt**	**try**	same	opposite
6. **predator**	**hunter**	same	opposite
7. **enemy**	**friend**	same	opposite
8. **arrive**	**come**	same	opposite

Find the Friend

READ the clues. Then WRITE the friend's name under each picture.

Darla is tall and thin.

Joe has curly black hair.

Kira wears the same shirt as Darla.

Talia is facing the opposite direction.

Larry is the opposite of Darla.

Who am I?

| 1 | 2 | 3 | 4 | 5 |

Criss Cross

READ the clues. FILL IN the boxes with the right word for each clue.

Across

2. Same as *come*
4. Opposite of *tiny*
5. Opposite of *succeed*

Down

1. Same as *pretty*
3. Opposite of *buddy*

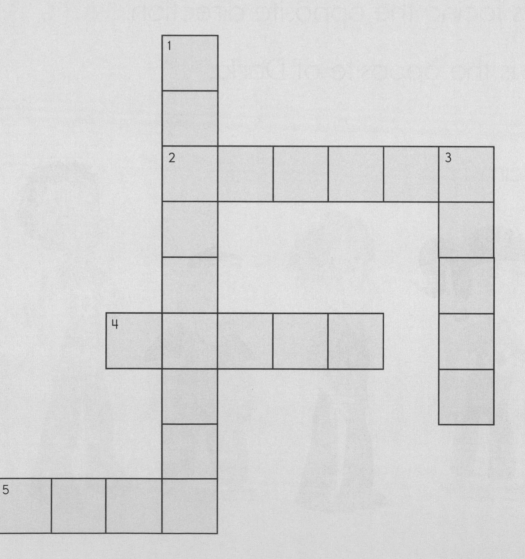

Dictionary Dare

Did you see that the word *giant* had two definitions in the Word List? Some words have more than one meaning. A dictionary gives all the meanings of a word.

READ the definition. Then ANSWER the questions.

skate—skayt 1. *noun* a shoe with a sharp blade that helps you slide on ice 2. *noun* a shoe with wheels that help you roll on the sidewalk 3. *verb* to use skates to move along the ground or on ice

1. How many meanings does *skate* have? _____

2. Is *skate* ever an adjective? Circle one: YES   NO

3. Use *skate* in a sentence as a verb. _____

_____

_____

_____

_____.

Word List

Compound words are made by putting two words together.

READ the words and their meanings.

base·ball—BAYS-bahl 1. *noun* a game played with a bat, a ball, and four bases 2. *noun* a ball used for playing baseball

bath·room—BATH-room *noun* a room for bathing and using the toilet

eve·ry·where—EHV-ree-wehr *adverb* in all places

light·house—LIT-hows *noun* a tall building with a big light that helps boats see the shore

side·walk—SID-wawk *noun* a smooth, hard walkway

stop·light—STAHP-lit *noun* a light that helps move traffic safely where two roads cross

sun·rise—SUHN-riz *noun* the time of day when the sun comes up

tooth·paste—TOOTH-payst *noun* a cream used to clean teeth

Match the Meaning

WRITE the words next to their definitions. LOOK at the word box for help.

| baseball | bathroom | everywhere | sunrise |
| lighthouse | sidewalk | stoplight | toothpaste |

1. _____ all over the world

2. _____ the very beginning of the day

3. _____ a game played with a bat

4. _____ a walkway

5. _____ a guide for ships at sea

6. _____ what you use to brush your teeth

7. _____ where you find a toilet

8. _____ a traffic light at a corner

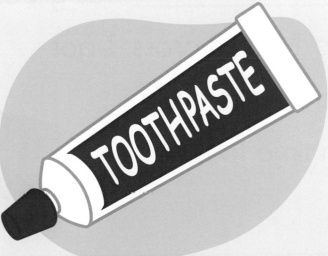

Finish the Story

READ the story. FILL IN the blanks with words from the word box.

| bathroom | baseball | sidewalk | stoplight | sunrise | toothpaste |

Just in Time

I got up at _____ to play _____
1   2
with my pals. As I raced to get ready, I dripped

_____ from my brush onto the floor in
3

the _____. Mom wasn't up yet, so I didn't
4

clean it. I grabbed my bat and ran down the

_____ to the corner. Luckily the
5

_____ was green,
6

so I could cross. I got

to the park just

in time to bat!

Add It Up

ADD UP the smaller words to make compound words that match the definitions.

Example: *light + house = lighthouse*
a light that helps keep ships safe

1. **grand** + _____ = _____

your mother's father

2. _____ + **board** = _____

a board with wheels used to roll down the sidewalk

3. _____ + **ground** = _____

a place with slides and swings

4. _____ + _____ = _____

a paper filled with the news of the day

5. **green** + _____ = _____

a building to keep plants warm

Night and Day

DRAW a line to match each word under the moon to its opposite under the sun.

HINT: Don't forget to use a dictionary.

sunrise	nothing
troublemaker	playtime
somebody	sunset
downstairs	daytime
nighttime	sidewalk
everything	upstairs
bedtime	peacemaker
highway	nobody

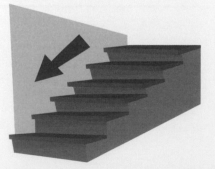
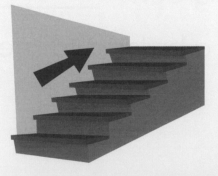

Cross Out

CROSS OUT the words that are NOT compound words.

1. starfish   football   adjective   predator

2. enemy   playground   everybody   arrive

3. lighthouse   beautiful   dictionary   blueberry

4. stoplight   unhappy   nothing   syllable

Parts of the Body

Word List

READ the words and their meanings.

braid—brayd 1. *noun* hair in a rope-like style 2. *verb* to put hair in a rope-like style

cheek—cheek *noun* the side of your face between your nose and your ear. You have two cheeks.

eye·brow—I-brow *noun* the strip of hair above your eye

freck·les—FREHK-lz *noun* spots on skin from the sun

frown—frown 1. *noun* a sad or mad face, the opposite of a smile 2. *verb* to make a sad or mad face

mouth—mowth 1. *noun* the hole in your face where you put your food 2. *verb* to talk with your lips without making a sound

stom·ach—STUHM-uhk *noun* your tummy, or belly, that tells you when you're hungry or full

throat—throht 1. *noun* the front part of your neck 2. *noun* the tube inside your neck that goes to your stomach and your lungs

Match the Meaning

WRITE the words next to their definitions. LOOK at the word box for help.

braid	eyebrow	frown	stomach
cheek	freckles	mouth	throat

1. _____ the opposite of *smile*

2. _____ the front of your neck

3. _____ where your lips and teeth are

4. _____ a rope-like ponytail

5. _____ spots on your skin

6. _____ the strip of hair above your eye

7. _____ the place where food goes after

you put it in your mouth

8. _____ the side of your face below

your eye

Criss Cross

READ the clues. FILL IN the boxes with the right word for each clue.

Across

3. The front of your neck
5. The side of your face

Down

1. The opposite of a smile
2. Your tummy
4. Spots on skin

Cross Out

CROSS OUT the words that are **not** parts of the body.

1. finger	throat	verb	definition
2. sunrise	fail	freckles	mouth
3. arm	sidewalk	stomach	attempt
4. syllable	eyebrow	giant	cheek

Parts of the Body

Find the Friend

READ the clues. Then WRITE the friend's name under each picture.

Doug has freckles on his cheeks.

Carly has two braids.

Tyara is frowning.

Jordan has the biggest eyebrows.

Connor has his mouth open.

Who am I?

| 1 | 2 | 3 | 4 | 5 |

Blank Out

FILL IN the blanks with the correct words for each part of the picture.

1. _____

2. _____

3. _____

4. _____

5. _____

6. _____

Word List

READ the words and their meanings.

breathe—bree*th verb* to take in air through your mouth or nose

chew—choo *verb* to use your teeth to bite food in your mouth

ex·er·cise—EHK-ser-siz 1. *noun* a set of moves that work out your body 2. *noun* an activity that helps practice a lesson 3. *verb* to move your body to make it strong and fit

kneel—neel *verb* to get down on your knees

reach—reech 1. *verb* to put out your hand to get something 2. *verb* to arrive at a place

shiv·er—SHIHV-er 1. *noun* a shake of the body 2. *verb* to shake your body, like when it's cold

squirm—skwerm *verb* to move around in a twisty-turny way

swal·low—SWAHL-oh *verb* to let food go from your mouth into your throat and stomach

Match the Meaning

WRITE the words next to their definitions. LOOK at the word box for help.

breathe	exercise	reach	squirm
chew	kneel	shiver	swallow

1. _____ to twist and turn

2. _____ to get down on your knees

3. _____ to shake

4. _____ to bite something in your mouth

5. _____ to put food down your throat

6. _____ to put out your hand

7. _____ to suck in air

8. _____ to help your body stay in shape

Right or Wrong?

UNDERLINE the sentence that matches the picture.

1.

Maddy is chewing gum.

Maddy is choosing gum.

2.

Mr. Santos is exiting.

Mr. Santos is exercising.

3.

Ty kicks on the ground.

Ty kneels on the ground.

4.

The baby reaches for her bottle.

The baby reads for her bottle.

Blank Out

FINISH each sentence with a word from the word box.

| breathe | exercise | reach | squirming |
| chew | kneel | shiver | swallow |

1. It was so cold out, I started to _____.

2. Mom goes to the gym to _____.

3. Ivan is too short to_____ the sink.

4. Aunt Didi always tells me to stop _____ and sit still.

5. My throat was so sore, it hurt to _____.

6. I have to _____ down to look under my bed.

7. If you don't have teeth, how do you _____?

8. When I get nervous, my mom always tell me, "Just _____."

Dictionary Dare

LOOK UP the words in a dictionary. Then WRITE the word from the word box that means something similar.

| beautiful | chew | reach | squirm |
| breathe | enemy | shiver | swallow |

1. wriggle _____

2. inhale _____

3. gorgeous _____

4. stretch _____

5. quake _____

6. gulp _____

7. gnaw _____

8. foe _____

Word Pictures

COLOR the spaces that show **verbs**.

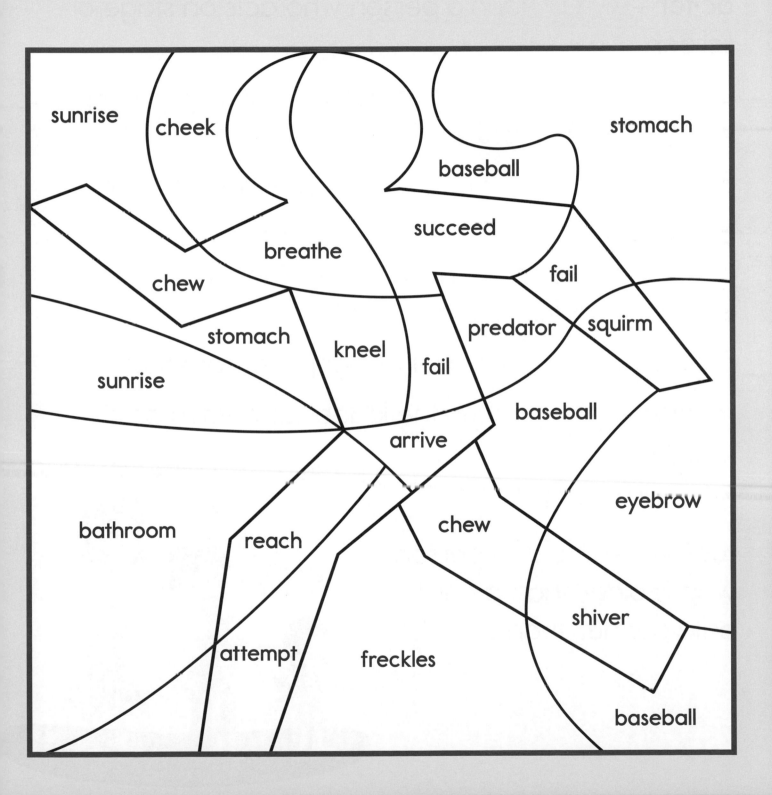

sunrise

cheek

stomach

baseball

succeed

breathe

fail

chew

stomach

kneel

predator

squirm

sunrise

fail

baseball

arrive

bathroom

eyebrow

reach

chew

shiver

attempt

freckles

baseball

Word List

READ the words and their meanings.

ac·tor—AK-ter *noun* a person who acts on stage or screen

a·dult—uh-DUHLT 1. *noun* a person who is grown up 2. *adjective* fully grown

bar·ber—BAHR-ber *noun* a person who cuts hair

cap·tain—KAP-tihn 1. *noun* the leader of a sports team 2. *noun* the leader of a ship or airplane 3. *noun* the leader of firefighters, police, or the military

crowd—krowd *noun* a lot of people all together

may·or—MAY-er *noun* the leader of a town or city

neigh·bor—NAY-ber *noun* a person who lives next door to or near you

teen—teen *noun* a person who is older than a child but younger than an adult

Match the Meaning

WRITE the words next to their definitions. LOOK at the word box for help.

actor	barber	crowd	neighbor
adult	captain	mayor	teen

1. _____ older than a child, but younger than an adult

2. _____ someone who is all grown up

3. _____ a large group of people

4. _____ the star of a movie

5. _____ someone who cuts your hair

6. _____ the leader of the city

7. _____ the head of the team

8. _____ a person in the next house

Finish the Story

READ the story. FILL IN the blanks with words from the box.

HINT: Read the whole story before you fill in the blanks.

actor	barber	captain	crowd	mayor	neighbor

Big Game? Big Deal!

Yesterday, I saw a _____ of about one hundred people in front of City Hall. One of them was Mr. Tilcio, the _____ of Folksburg. He gave a big medal to Sara Wells. Sara is the _____ of our soccer team. Mr. Tilcio also gave a medal to Rick Randall, the _____ who stars in Folksburg Follies. But he gave the biggest medal to Mr. Sateen, the _____ who cuts my dad's hair! I couldn't believe it. But my next-door _____ told me that Mr. Sateen saved a baby from a fire. Wow!

Criss Cross

READ the clues. FILL IN the boxes with the right word for each clue.

Across

2. A 15-year-old
4. A grown up
5. A haircutter

Down

1. Someone who lives next door
3. Leader of a town or city

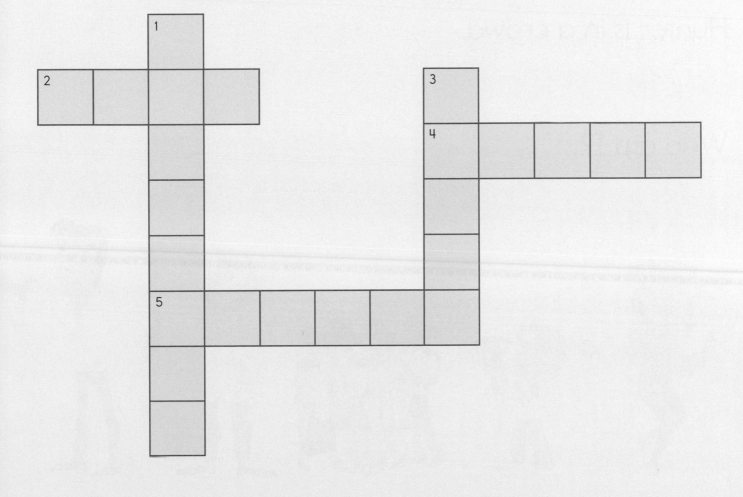

Find the Friend

READ the clues. Then WRITE the friend's name under each picture.

Cyrus is a barber.

Leena is a teen.

Bart is an actor.

Serena is captain of her team.

Hunter is in a crowd.

Who am I?

| 1 | 2 | 3 | 4 | 5 |

Maze Crazy!

DRAW a line through the words for **people** to help the boy get to the crowd.

Start at the green arrow.

START

milk

elephant

neighbor

pig

cow

captain

mayor

corn

neighbor

actor

goat

teen

monkey

football

milk

barber

sheep

everywhere

ham

playground

captain

eggs

adult

END

People Actions

Word List

READ the words and their meanings.

a·gree—uh-GREE 1. *verb* to think the same way as someone else 2. *verb* to say yes to something

bor·row—BAHR-oh *verb* when someone allows you to take something for a short time, then give it back

ex·plain—ihk-SPLAYN *verb* to tell or teach someone about something

for·give—fer-GIHV *verb* to stop being mad and make up after a fight with someone

fright·en—FRIT-uhn *verb* to scare somebody

re·spect—rih-SPEHKT 1. *noun* a feeling that you honor someone 2. *verb* to honor and show consideration for someone

share—shehr 1. *noun* one person's part of something that can be split 2. *verb* to let other people use your things or eat your food 3. *verb* to use something with other people

sug·gest—suhg-JEHST 1. *verb* to hint at something 2. *verb* to give an idea or plan as an option

Match the Meaning

WRITE the words next to their definitions. LOOK at the word box for help.

agree	explain	frighten	share
borrow	forgive	respect	suggest

1. _____ to honor someone

2. _____ to let someone use your toys

3. _____ to check out a book from

the library

4. _____ to make someone understand

5. _____ to offer an idea

6. _____ to say yes

7. _____ to scare someone

8. _____ to make up and forget a fight

Right or Wrong?

UNDERLINE the sentence that matches the picture.

1.

   Tom respects Donna.

   Tom does not respect Donna.

2.

   Jean shares her pizza with Mike.

   Jean won't share her pizza with Mike.

3.

   Sondra frightens Neal.

   Sondra forgets Neal.

4.

   Neal forgives Sondra.

   Neal suggests Sondra.

Dictionary Dare

LOOK UP the words in a dictionary. Then WRITE the word from the word box that means the **opposite**.

explain	enemy	agree	respect
beautiful	share	borrow	neighbor

1. loan _____

2. confuse _____

3. disrespect _____

4. hideous _____

5. hoard _____

6. foreigner _____

7. ally _____

8. disagree _____

People Actions

Blank Out

FINISH each sentence with a word from the word box.

| agree | explain | frighten | shares |
| borrow | forgive | respect | suggests |

1. Miles didn't understand the rules, so I tried to

   _____.

2. I will never _____ Sylvia for calling me a geek!

3. It's important to _____ the police.

4. Donna _____ that we play in the tree

   house today.

5. Mom thinks I should go to bed, but I don't

   _____.

6. Taffy never _____ her popcorn at the movies.

7. Bill tried to _____ me with his

   mask, but I wasn't scared.

8. Can I _____ your video

   game for a few days?

Cross Out

CROSS OUT the words that are NOT verbs.

1. enemy   beautiful   forgive   attempt

2. frighten   scary   exercise   definition

3. verb   share   throat   borrow

4. respect   sidewalk   suggest   idea

Family

Word List

READ the words and their meanings.

aunt—ant 1. *noun* the sister of your mother or father 2. *noun* the wife of your uncle

broth·er—BRUH*TH*-er *noun* a boy whose mother and father have another child

grand·fa·ther—GRAND-fah-*ther* 1. *noun* the father of your father or mother 2. *noun* your grandmother's husband

grand·moth·er—GRAND-muh*th*-er 1. *noun* the mother of your father or mother 2. *noun* your grandfather's wife

hus·band—HUHZ-buhnd *noun* a man who is married

sis·ter—SIHS-ter *noun* a girl whose mother and father have another child

un·cle—UHNG-kuhl 1. *noun* the brother of your mother or father 2. *noun* the husband of your aunt

wife—wif *noun* a woman who is married

Match the Meaning

WRITE the words next to their definitions. LOOK at the word box for help.

| aunt | husband | brother | sister |
| grandfather | uncle | grandmother | wife |

1. _____ a man who is married

2. _____ your grandmother's husband

3. _____ another child (girl) of your parents

4. _____ your aunt's husband

5. _____ a woman who is married

6. _____ another child (boy) of your parents

7. _____ your uncle's wife

8. _____ your grandfather's wife

Criss Cross

READ the clues. FILL IN the boxes with the right word for each clue.

HINT: You might have to look up some words in the clues.

Across

2. Your parent's father
3. A male spouse

Down

1. A male sibling

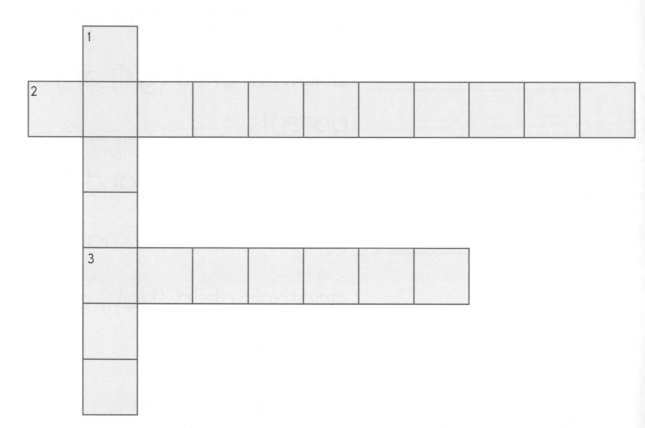

What do these words mean?

parent _____

sibling _____

spouse _____

Blank Out

FILL IN the blanks for each part of the family tree with the words in the word box. Use each word just once.

aunt	brother	grandfather	husband
uncle	sister	grandmother	wife

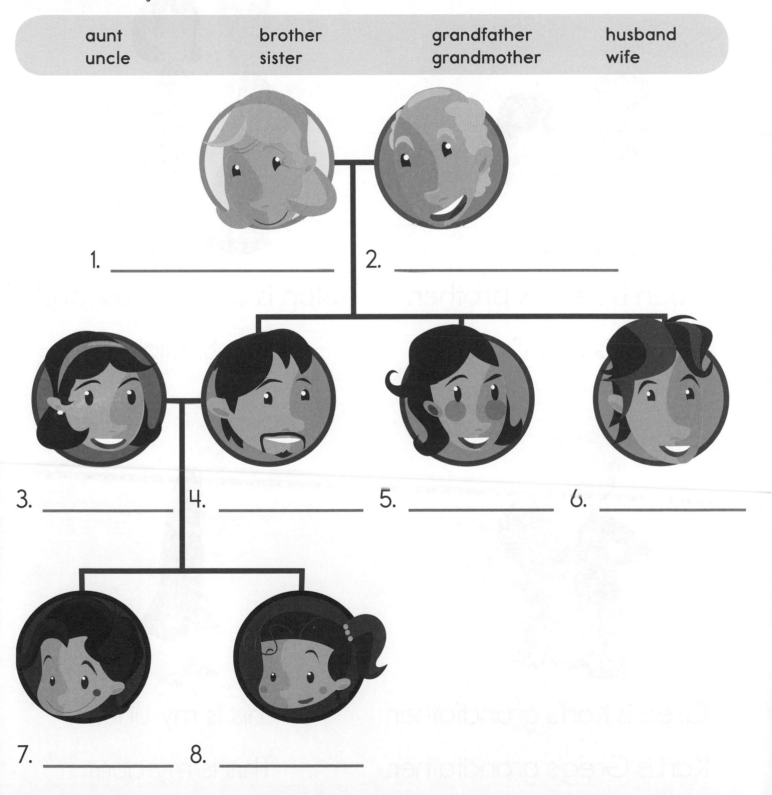

1. _____

2. _____

3. _____

4. _____

5. _____

6. _____

7. _____

8. _____

Family

Right or Wrong?

UNDERLINE the sentence that matches the picture.

1.

Jen is Peter's brother.

Jen is Peter's sister.

2.

Stan is Sheila's husband.

Stan is Sheila's wife.

3.

Greg is Karl's grandfather.

Karl is Greg's grandfather.

4.

This is my uncle.

This is my aunt.

Cross Out

CROSS OUT the words that do **not** name family members.

1. grandfather   daughter   frighten   frown

2. son   bathroom   suggest   sister

3. predator   agree   mother   aunt

4. respect   uncle   brother   elephant

Word List

READ the words and their meanings.

base·ment—BAS-muhnt *noun* a room or rooms under a house or building

clos·et—CLAHZ-iht *noun* a very small room to keep clothes and shoes

com·fort·a·ble—KUHM-fer-tuh-buhl 1. *adjective* very soft or easy 2. *adjective* with no pain or fear

emp·ty—EHMP-tee *adjective* having nothing inside

fa·vor·ite—FA-ver-iht *adjective* the one that is liked the most

lawn—lawn *noun* the grass around a house

paint—peynt 1. *noun* color that can be put on walls or objects 2. *verb* to put color on something using paint

re·frig·er·a·tor—rih-FRIHJ-uh-ray-ter *noun* a metal box that keeps food and drinks cold

Match the Meaning

WRITE the words next to their definitions. LOOK at the word box for help.

basement	comfortable	favorite	paint
closet	empty	lawn	refrigerator

1. _____ the opposite of *full*

2. _____ a room just for coats and shoes

3. _____ the place under the house

4. _____ the one you like the best

5. _____ where you put food to keep

   it cold

6. _____ what makes the color on

   the walls

7. _____ nice and warm

   and soft

8. _____ a yard full of grass

Finish the Story

READ the story. FILL IN the blanks with words from the word box.

| comfortable | empty | favorite | lawn | refrigerator |

Bad Day

What a bad day! When I was hungry, the

_____ was _____.
₁ ₂

There was nothing to eat! When I turned on the

TV, my _____ show was over.
₃

So I went to take a nap. Just when I got

_____ on my bed, my brother started
₄

to mow the _____.
₅

It was too loud to sleep!

I hope tomorrow is better.

Criss Cross

READ the clues. FILL IN the boxes with the right word for each clue.

Across

3. A room for clothes
4. Nothing inside
5. A grassy place

Down

1. Put color on walls
2. The lowest room

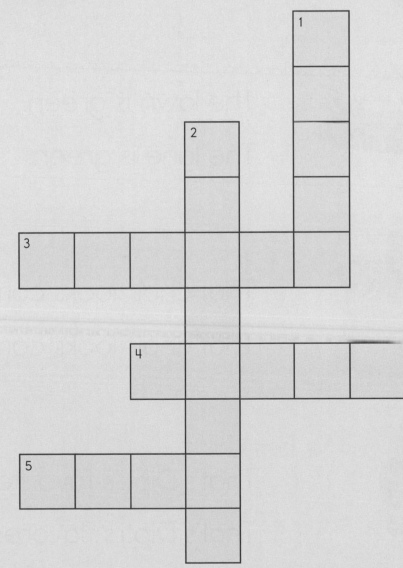

Right or Wrong?

UNDERLINE the sentence that matches the picture.

1.

The box is empty.

The box is easy.

2.

The lawn is green.

The lane is green.

3.

That chair looks compatible.

That chair looks comfortable.

4.

That's Dipti's favorite doll.

That's Dipti's flavored doll.

Maze Crazy!

DRAW a line through the **adjectives** to get to the smiley face.
Start at the yellow arrow.

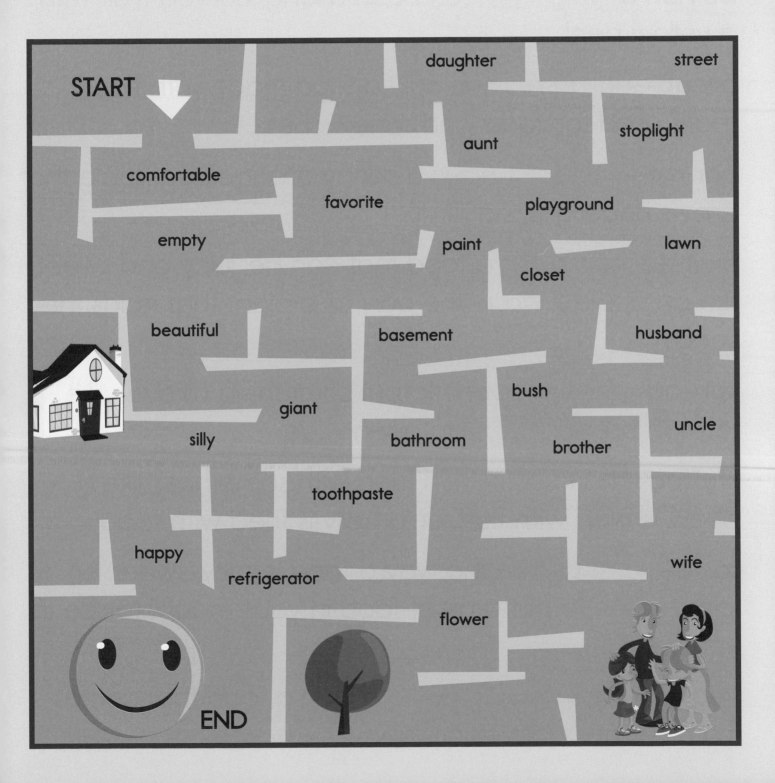

START

daughter

street

comfortable

aunt

stoplight

favorite

playground

empty

paint

lawn

closet

beautiful

basement

husband

bush

giant

uncle

silly

bathroom

brother

toothpaste

happy

wife

refrigerator

flower

END

Word List

READ the words and their meanings.

ba·nan·a—buh-NAN-uh *noun* a long, curved fruit with a yellow peel

bread—brehd *noun* a baked food made with flour that's used for toast and sandwiches

car·rot—KEHR-uht *noun* a skinny orange vegetable that grows underground

fruit—froot 1. *noun* a food that can be juicy and sweet, like an apple 2. *noun* the part of a plant that holds the seeds

spread—sprehd 1. *verb* to put something all over, like jam on bread 2. *verb* to open wide

stuffed—stuhft *adjective* filled with something, like a pillow is filled with fluff, or a belly is filled with food

taste—tayst 1. *noun* the way a food is salty, sweet, or icky 2. *verb* to put a bit of food in your mouth to see if you like it

veg·e·ta·ble—VEHJ-tuh-buhl *noun* a food that comes from a plant's leaves or roots

Match the Meaning

WRITE the words next to their definitions. LOOK at the word box for help.

| banana | carrot | spread | taste |
| bread | fruit | stuffed | vegetable |

1. _____ to try a bite of food

2. _____ an orange vegetable

3. _____ a fruit with a yellow peel

4. _____ the leaves or roots of a plant that you can eat

5. _____ very full of something

6. _____ part of the plant that has seeds

7. _____ to put something all over

8. _____ food that turns into toast

Find the Friend

READ the clues. Then WRITE the friend's name under each picture.

Shama is eating a fruit.

Mai has bananas on her shirt.

Crispin is eating vegetables.

Val has carrots on her shirt.

Lyle is eating bread.

Who am I?

| 1 | 2 | 3 | 4 | 5 |

Dictionary Dare

LOOK UP these foods in a dictionary. Then CIRCLE if it's a fruit or a vegetable.

1. **potato**   fruit   vegetable

2. **spinach**   fruit   vegetable

3. **cherry**   fruit   vegetable

4. **pear**   fruit   vegetable

5. **lettuce**   fruit   vegetable

6. **broccoli**   fruit   vegetable

7. **peach**   fruit   vegetable

8. **onion**   fruit   vegetable

Blank Out

FINISH each sentence with a word from the word box.

| banana | carrots | spread | taste |
| bread | fruit | stuffed | vegetables |

1. Cartoon rabbits are always chomping on _____.

2. I love fish sticks, but Amy hates the way they _____.

3. Nadine helped Mom _____ frosting on the cake.

4. Isaac ate nothing but _____ and butter all day.

5. A tomato is really a _____ because it has seeds.

6. We were all _____ after Thanksgiving dinner.

7. Chloe peeled the _____ for the monkey to eat.

8. Saul eats his meat, but no leafy _____.

Word Pictures

COLOR the spaces that show words for **food** and **eating**.

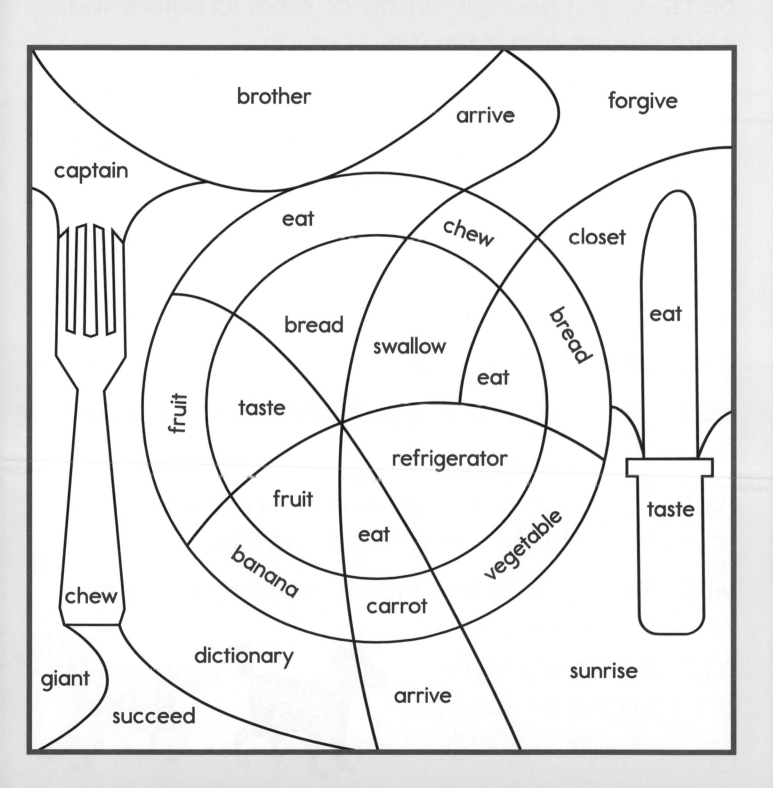

brother

arrive

forgive

captain

eat

chew

closet

fruit

bread

swallow

eat

bread

eat

taste

refrigerator

taste

fruit

eat

vegetable

chew

banana

carrot

dictionary

sunrise

giant

arrive

succeed

Word List

READ the words and their meanings.

beast—beest *noun* an animal or other creature that is not human and doesn't act human

crea·ture—KREE-cher *noun* a living animal or human

feath·er—FEH*TH*-er *noun* one of the soft pieces that cover a bird's body and wings

flight—flit 1. *noun* a trip through the air, like on a plane 2. *noun* a fast getaway, escape

flock—flahk 1. *noun* a group of birds 2. *verb* to make a group, like a flock of birds

herd—herd 1. *noun* a group of land animals like cows 2. *verb* to make a group of animals go somewhere

tame—taym 1. *adjective* quiet, safe, and nice 2. *verb* to make a wild animal be nice to humans

wild—wild 1. *adjective* not tame, not safe, not able to live with humans 2. *noun* a place where people don't live, like the jungle

Match the Meaning

WRITE the words next to their definitions. LOOK at the word box for help.

beast	feather	flock	tame
creature	flight	herd	wild

1. _____ a group of birds

2. _____ unsafe, not tame

3. _____ a creature that isn't human

4. _____ an air trip

5. _____ a human or an animal

6. _____ not a danger

7. _____ what you pluck from a bird

8. _____ a bunch of cows

Finish the Story

READ the story. FILL IN the blanks with words from the word box.

beasts	feathers	flocks	herds	tame	wild

A Trip to Africa

Africa is home to many _____, like lions.
1

They're cats, but not like the _____ kitties
2

we have in our homes. Lions are _____
3

predators that may kill humans. In the skies above

Africa, you can see _____ of beautiful
4

birds with colorful _____. You might also
5

find giant _____
6

of elephants

walking for miles

to find water.

Criss Cross

READ the clues. FILL IN the boxes with the right word for each clue.

Across

1. Birds that fly together
3. A crowd of cows
4. A sky trip

Down

2. A living being
4. It's on a bird's wing

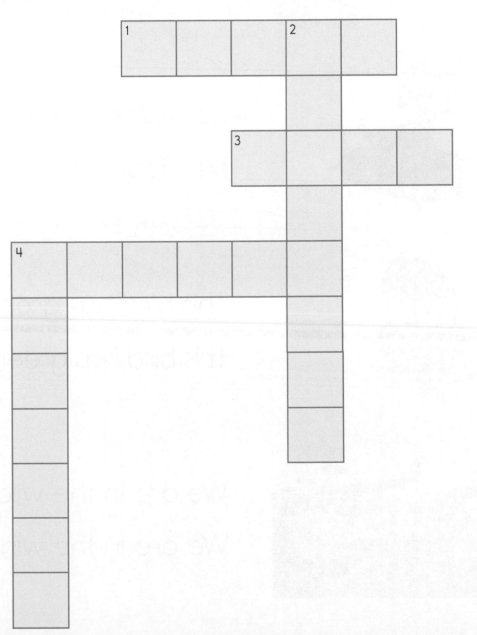

Right or Wrong?

UNDERLINE the sentence that matches the picture.

1.

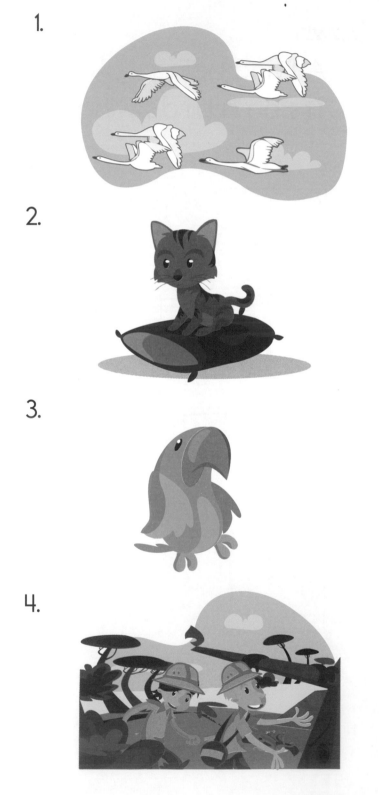

A herd of geese flew by.

A flock of geese flew by.

2.

Mr. Tibbles is tame.

Mr. Tibbles is wild.

3.

This bird has green fathers.

This bird has green feathers.

4.

We are in the wild.

We are in the wind.

Word Pictures

COLOR the spaces that show words for **parts of animals**.

HINT: Don't forget to look up any words you don't know.

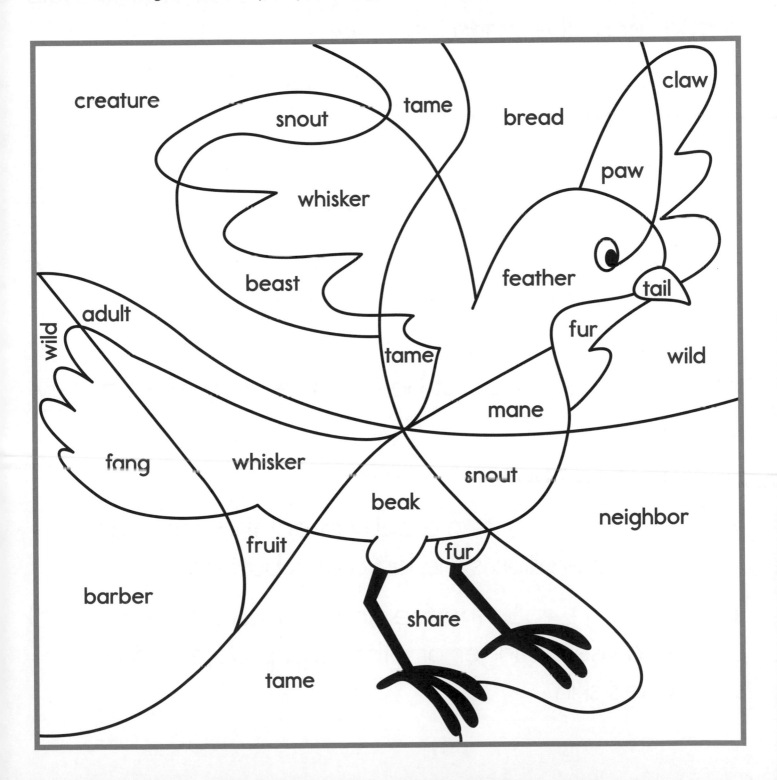

Word List

READ the words and their meanings.

an·ten·nae—an-TEHN-ee *noun* two thin feelers that help a bug sense the world

but·ter·fly—BUHT-er-fli *noun* an insect with large wings that are sometimes very colorful

cat·er·pil·lar—KAT-er-pihl-er *noun* an insect like a worm that turns into a butterfly or a moth

co·coon—kuh-KOON *noun* a silk wrap or bag made by an insect to keep its body or eggs safe. A caterpillar goes into a cocoon while turning into a moth.

hive—hiv *noun* a nest of bees, where they make honey

in·sect—IHN-sehkt *noun* a small creature with no backbone (a bug)

lar·va—LAHR-vuh *noun* a baby insect that looks like a worm. A caterpillar is the larva of a butterfly.

sting—stihng 1. *noun* the feeling of a bug bite or pin prick 2. *verb* to use a stinger or other sharp object to break someone's skin

Match the Meaning

WRITE the words in the box next to their definitions

antennae	caterpillar	hive	larva
butterfly	cocoon	insect	sting

1. _____ a safe, silky wrap

2. _____ a bug

3. _____ feelers

4. _____ the larva of a moth or butterfly

5. _____ a sharp pain

6. _____ an insect with big wings

7. _____ a baby bug

8. _____ where bees live

Find the Friend

READ the clues. Then WRITE the friend's name under each picture.

Binky is in a cocoon.

Slinky is a caterpillar.

Tinky lives in a hive.

Pinky is a butterfly.

Dinky has purple antennae.

Who am I?

| 1 | 2 | 3 | 4 | 5 |

Blank Out

FINISH each sentence with a word from the word box.

| antennae butterflies | caterpillars cocoon | hives insects | larva sting |

1. My arm still hurts from that bee _____.

2. Some bugs use their _____ to smell.

3. Teejay draws _____ with giant, beautiful wings.

4. That wormy maggot is the _____ of a fly.

5. Bears get honey from bee _____ they find in the trees.

6. Some insects put their eggs in a _____ to keep them safe.

7. I don't kill _____ because one day they'll be butterflies!

8. Nate loves nature, but he hates _____ that bite.

Criss Cross

READ the clues. FILL IN the boxes with the right word for each clue.

Across

2. A bug
5. A bug's feelers
6. A nest of bees

Down

1. A sharp pain
3. A safe, silky place
4. A baby bug

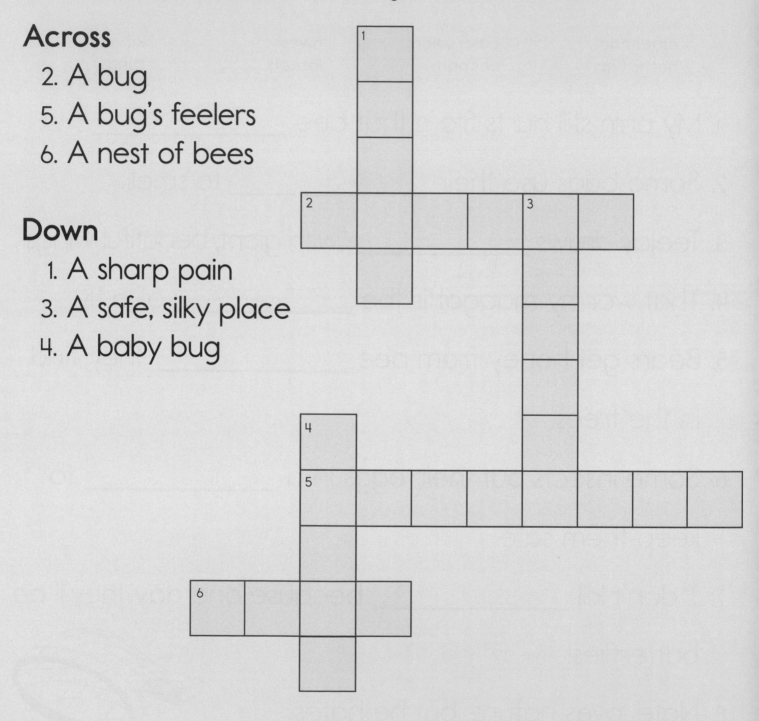

Maze Crazy!

DRAW a line through the words about **bugs** to get to the beehive.

Start at the green arrow.

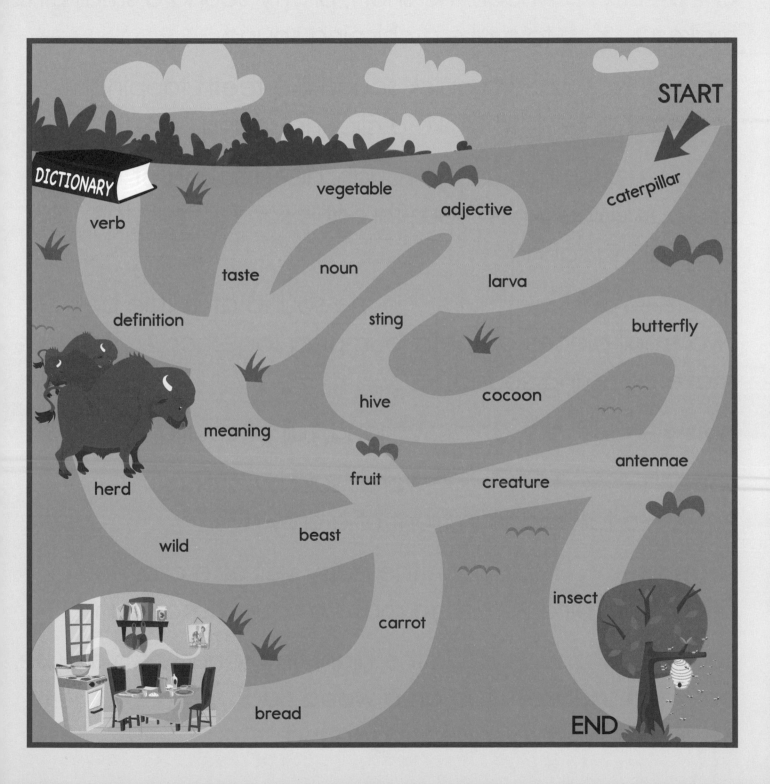

START

caterpillar

DICTIONARY

vegetable

adjective

verb

taste

noun

larva

butterfly

definition

sting

cocoon

hive

meaning

antennae

herd

fruit

creature

wild

beast

insect

carrot

bread

END

What's That Sound?

Word List

READ the words and their meanings.

chirp—cherp 1. *noun* the short, pretty sound a small bird makes 2. *verb* to make a chirping sound

click—klihk 1. *noun* a quick sound like teeth tapping together 2. *verb* to make a clicking sound

croak—krohk 1. *noun* the rough, deep sound of a frog, or your voice when your throat is sore 2. *verb* to make a croaking sound

jin·gle—JIHNG-guhl 1. *noun* the sound of a little bell, or two small pieces of metal bumping together 2. *verb* to make a jingling sound

nois·y—NOY-zee *adjective* loud, full of sound

speech—speech 1. *noun* words said by a person 2. *noun* a talk made in front of a crowd

squawk—skwahk 1. *noun* the noisy yell of a crow or other loud bird 2. *verb* to make a squawking sound

squeak—skweek 1. *noun* the high, tiny sound of a mouse, or when sneakers rub on a wood floor 2. *verb* to make a squeaking sound

Match the Meaning

WRITE the words next to their definitions. LOOK at the word box for help.

| click | croak | noisy | squawk |
| chirp | jingle | speech | squeak |

1. _____ loud

2. _____ the sound a little bird makes

3. _____ a high, tiny sound

4. _____ a sound like teeth tapping

   together

5. _____ the sound of a shaking bell

6. _____ words said out loud

7. _____ the yell of a loud bird

8. _____ the sound of a frog

What's That Sound?

Criss Cross

READ the clues. FILL IN the boxes with the right word for each clue.

Across

3. Your teeth can make this sound.
5. Full of sound
6. A mousy sound

Down

1. A sudden bird yell
2. Sounds like a tiny bell
4. A deep frog sound

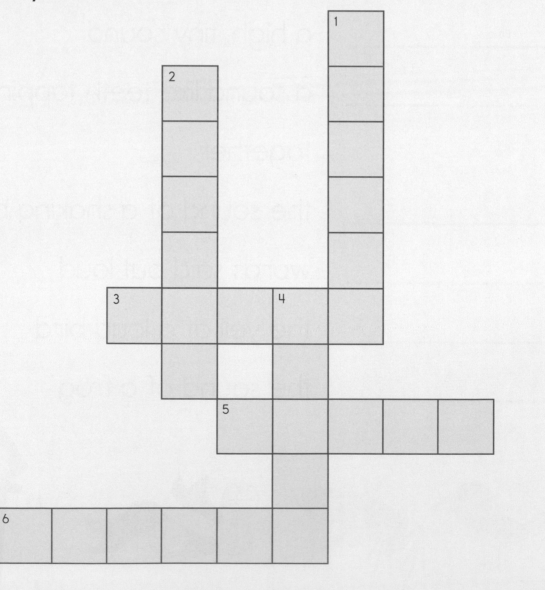

Blank Out

FINISH each sentence with a word from the word box.

| clicking | croak | noisy | squawks |
| chirping | jingle | speech | squeaking |

1. Ben had a bad cold, so his voice sounded like a
_____.

2. The crowd was talking and clapping. It was very
_____.

3. Jess says we have mice. She hears them
_____ in the walls.

4. Mom gave a long, boring _____ about
doing chores.

5. I shivered so hard, my teeth were _____
together.

6. Dad likes to _____ his keys while he walks
to the car.

7. The big parrot always _____ when I
come into the pet shop.

8. It was a nice morning.
The sun was shining and the
birds were _____.

What's That Sound?

Pick the One

CIRCLE the sound that fits best for each word.

1. **lion**   (roar)   squeak   speech

2. **dog toy**   crash   bark   squeak

3. **car horn**   bang   honk   buzz

4. **carrot**   chirp   squeak   crunch

5. **crow**   squawk   roar   bark

6. **push button**   shout   quack   click

7. **bird**   bark   chirp   roar

8. **frog**   speech   croak   squeak

Cross Out

CROSS OUT the words that are **not** sounds.

1. click   carrot   larva   hoot

2. paint   teen   roar   squawk

3. honk   chirp   taste   kneel

4. squeak   cheek   screech   frown

Word List

READ the words and their meanings.

crop—krahp *noun* a planting of something, like corn, that a farmer is growing in a field

field—feeld *noun* a wide space of ground that has plants growing in it, like grass or a crop

flood—fluhd 1. *noun* a lot of water that overflows from a river, or fills an area like a house 2. *verb* to fill an area with water

moun·tain—MOWN-tuhn *noun* a tall peak of land, much higher than a hill

nat·u·ral—NATCH-er-uhl 1. *adjective* the way nature made it, not changed by humans 2. *adjective* not fake

shade—shad *noun* a place where the sun is blocked by something, like under a tree

soil—soyl 1. *noun* dirt that is used for growing plants 2. *verb* to make something dirty

val·ley—VAL-ee *noun* a low spot between hills or mountains

Match the Meaning

WRITE the words in the box next to their definitions.

crop	flood	natural	soil
field	mountain	shade	valley

1. _____ a really tall hill

2. _____ a cool, dark spot

3. _____ a bunch of plants, like corn

4. _____ a low spot between hills

5. _____ a place to grow crops

6. _____ not changed

7. _____ a lot of water

8. _____ dirt

Nature

Blank Out!

FINISH each sentence with a word from the box.

crops	flooded	natural	soiled
field	mountain	shade	valley

1. The plastic tree in the living room doesn't look _____.

2. Next to our house is a big _____ full of weeds.

3. On a hot day, it's nice to sit in the _____ of a tree.

4. We live in a deep _____ that follows a river.

5. After Zan walked in the mud, his socks were all _____.

6. Farmer Ned grows three _____: corn, wheat, and oats.

7. Last year, my Uncle Jaime climbed a tall _____.

8. We had to stay in a hotel because our house _____ in the storm.

Right or Wrong?

UNDERLINE the sentence that matches the picture.

1.

Vernon is sitting in the shake.

Vernon is sitting in the shade.

2.

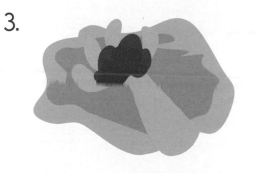

Corn is growing in this field.

Corn is growing in this feel.

3.

This soil is good for growing things.

This soap is good for growing things.

4.

The house is on the mountain.

The house is in the valley.

Same or Opposite?

READ each word pair. CIRCLE if they are the same or opposites.

HINT: Look up any words you don't know.

1. **mountain**   valley   same   opposite

2. **fake**   natural   same   opposite

3. **soil**   dirt   same   opposite

4. **field**   meadow   same   opposite

5. **natural**   unchanged   same   opposite

6. **flooded**   dry   same   opposite

7. **soiled**   clean   same   opposite

8. **shady**   sunny   same   opposite

Word Pictures

COLOR the spaces that show words for things in nature.

HINT: Don't forget to look up any words you don't know.

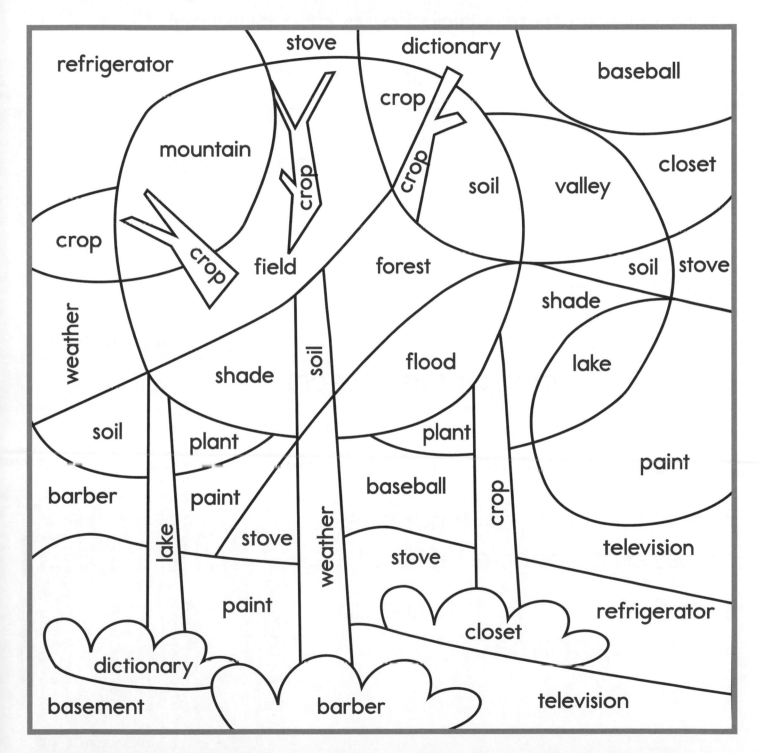

Word List

READ the words and their meanings.

el·e·va·tor—EHL-uh-vay-ter *noun* a moving box that takes you up to the high floors of a building

lit·ter—LIHT-er 1. *noun* trash that is on the ground 2. *verb* to leave trash on the ground

lone·ly—LOHN-lee *adjective* sad because there's nobody around

mod·ern—MAHD-dern *adjective* very new and up to date, not old

mon·u·ment—MAHN-yuh-muhnt *noun* anything that is put up to honor a person or event

neigh·bor·hood—NAY-ber-hud *noun* an area where people live

rude—rood *adjective* not nice, makes other people feel bad

spend—spehnd *verb* to use up, like money or time

Match the Meaning

WRITE the words next to their definitions. LOOK at the word box for help.

elevator	lonely	monument	rude
litter	modern	neighborhood	spend

1. _____ the area where you live

2. _____ to leave trash on the street

3. _____ not old fashioned

4. _____ a box that takes you up

5. _____ to use up

6. _____ sad and alone

7. _____ something to honor a person

8. _____ not nice

Finish the Story

READ the story. FILL IN the blanks with words from the box.

| elevator | modern | neighborhood | spend |
| lonely | monument | rude | |

A New Friend

I get a little _____ in the summer when all

the kids in my _____ go to camp. I

1

_____ a lot of time playing at the park

2

_____ a lot of time playing at the park

3

by myself. There's a _____ there, of a big,

4

stone soldier. One day, I saw a girl sitting on the

soldier's foot. At first she was _____ and

5

wouldn't talk to me. But now we hang out all the

time! She lives in a new, _____ apartment

6

building with an _____ to take

7

you to her floor. I hope we stay

friends when the summer is over!

Criss Cross

READ the clues. FILL IN the boxes with the right word for each clue.

HINT: Look up words you don't know.

Across

1. New
2. By yourself and sad
3. Lets you skip the stairs

Down

1. A statue that honors someone
2. Trash on the street

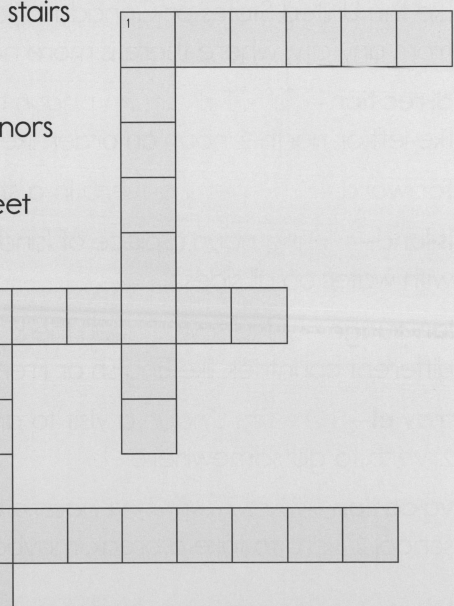

Word List

READ the words and their meanings.

back·ward—BAK-werd 1. *adverb* back in the direction you came from 2. *adjective* pointing the wrong way, so the front is facing back

coun·try—KUHN-tree 1. *noun* the nation where you live, like the United States or Canada 2. *noun* a place far away from any city, where there is more nature

di·rec·tion—duh-REHK-shuhn 1. *noun* the way you're going, like left or north 2. *noun* an order, like "go to bed now"

for·ward—FOR-werd *adverb* in a straight direction

is·land—I-luhnd *noun* a piece of land that is in the ocean, with water on all sides

lan·guage—LANG-gwihj *noun* the kind of speech used in different countries, like English or French

trav·el—TRAV-uhl 1. *noun* a visit to another place 2. *verb* to go somewhere

va·ca·tion—vay-KAY-shuhn 1. *noun* a break from work or school 2. *verb* to take a break, maybe travel

Match the Meaning

WRITE the words next to their definitions. LOOK at the word box for help.

backward	direction	island	travel
country	forward	language	vacation

1. _____ like France or England

2. _____ land with water all around

3. _____ the opposite of *forward*

4. _____ to take a trip

5. _____ an order from someone

6. _____ time off from work

7. _____ keep going straight

8. _____ what speech you use

Find the Friend

READ the clues. Then WRITE the friends' names next to the corresponding numbers.

Jorge lives in the country of France.

Chantal's shirt is backward.

Simon lives on an island.

Fiona is traveling.

Mona is on vacation in Germany.

Who am I?

1. _____

2. _____

3. _____

4. _____

5. _____

Blank Out

FINISH each sentence with a word from the word box.

| backward country | directions forward | islands language | traveled vacation |

1. In chorus, we have to face _____ and smile at the crowd.

2. At our school, we get two months of _____ in the summer.

3. I'm from India. What _____ are you from?

4. Last year, my uncle _____ all over the world!

5. People who look _____ when they walk will bump into things.

6. Hawaii is a string of _____.

7. North, south, east, and west are all _____ on a map.

8. Sometimes I think my math teacher is speaking another _____.

Whole Wide World

Right or Wrong?

UNDERLINE the sentence that matches the picture.

1. Staci is walking forward.

   Staci is walking backward.

2. Martin is on an island.

   Martin is on a mountain.

3. ZIPPLE-BOP!! WQU SNORKYT.

   Xyqx speaks a different langor.

   Xyqx speaks a different language.

4. Joel is in the country.

   Joel is in the city.

Maze Crazy!

DRAW a line through words about **travel** to get to the train.
Start at the green arrow.

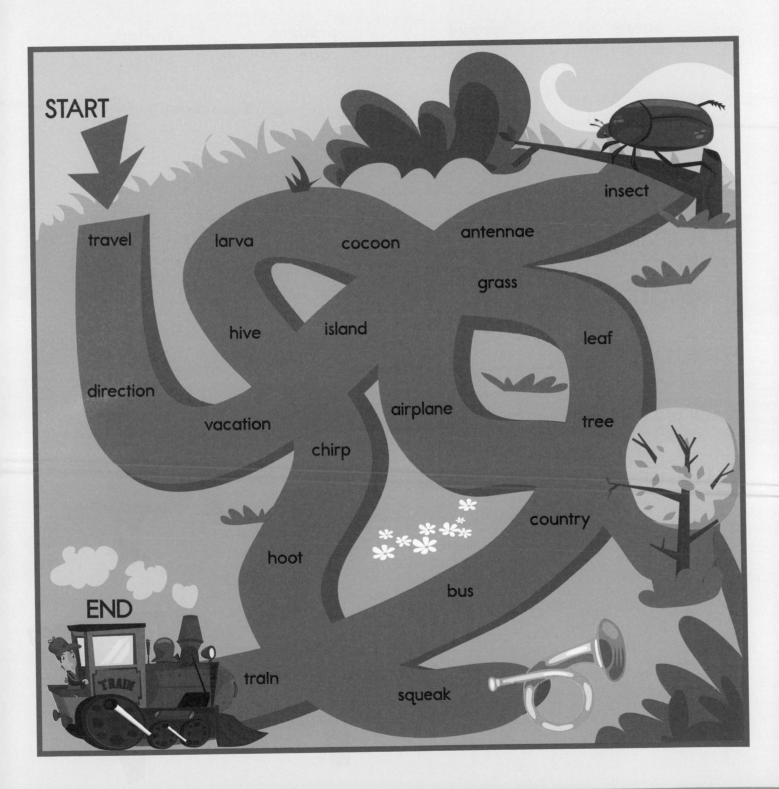

START

travel   larva   cocoon   antennae   insect

grass

hive   island   leaf

direction   airplane   tree

vacation

chirp

country

hoot   bus

END   train   squeak

Dictionary Dare

LOOK UP the words in a dictionary. Then FILL IN the blanks with words from the box that mean the **opposite**.

| agree | crowd | predator | stuffed |
| basement | noise | rude | tame |

1. individual _____

2. attic _____

3. starving _____

4. savage _____

5. refuse _____

6. prey _____

7. polite _____

8. silence _____

THE ART OF ROME
French History
The Amazon Rainforest
Algo
Space Exploration
World Atlas

Reference Section

Blank Out

FINISH each sentence with a word from the word box.

| adjectives | country | dictionary | opposite |
| compound | definition | language | verb |

1. Canada is a _____.

2. *Pretty* and *purple* are _____.

3. Every word has a _____.

4. You can look up a word's meaning in the

   _____.

5. A word that names an action is a _____.

6. *Night* is the _____ of *day*.

7. *Lighthouse* is a

   _____ word.

8. English is a _____.

Review

Pick the One

READ each sentence. CIRCLE the correct part of speech for each word in green.

HINT: Some words are tricky because they can be nouns, verbs, or adjectives!

1. That man littered the sidewalk with his lunch bag.

noun   verb   adjective

2. This is Gerri's second attempt at that skateboard trick.

noun   verb   adjective

3. The door clicked as it slid open.

noun   verb   adjective

4. Mom cried when she saw our flooded basement.

noun   verb   adjective

5. Do you have time to braid my hair?

noun   verb   adjective

6. All the kids flock around the ice cream truck when it comes.

noun   verb   adjective

7. Can I have a taste of that cake?

noun   verb   adjective

Cross Out

CROSS OUT the words that are **not** nouns.

1. comfortable   monument   forgive   toothpaste

2. flight   lonely   stomach   borrow

3. succeed   wife   basement   empty

4. arrive   elevator   rude   neighborhood

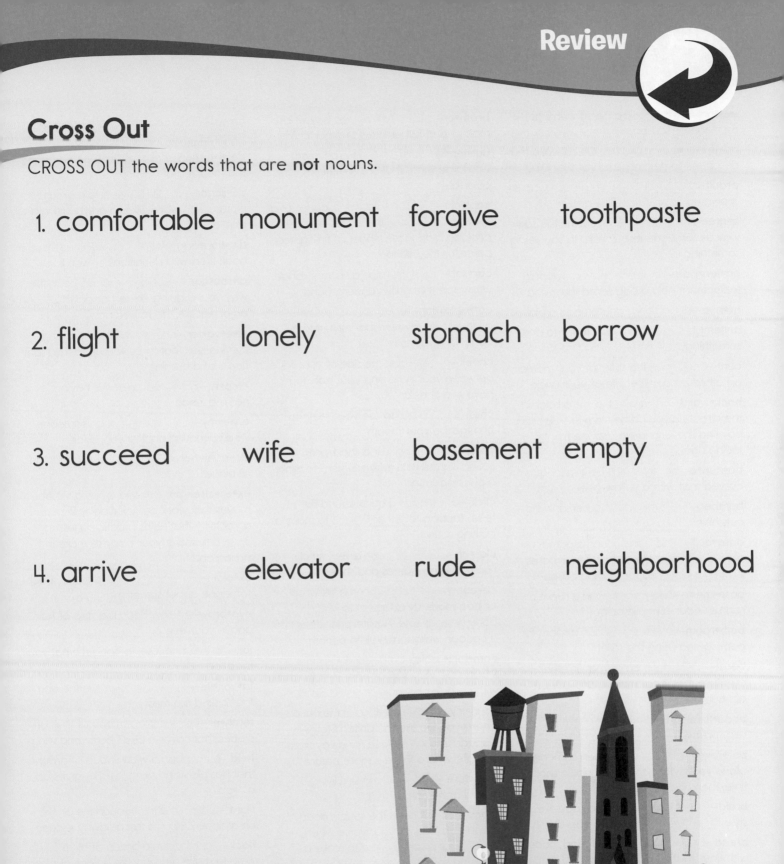

Index

ac•tor—AK-ter *noun* a person who acts on stage or screen

ad•jec•tive—AJ-ihk-tihv *noun* a word that describes something, like *pretty* or *blue*

a•dult—uh-DUHLT 1. *noun* a person who is grown up 2. *adjective* fully grown

a•gree—uh-GREE 1. *verb* to think the same way as someone else 2. *verb* to say yes to something

an•ten•nae—an-TEHN-ee *noun* two thin feelers that help a bug sense the world

ar•rive—uh-RIV *verb* to come to a place

at•tempt—uh-TEHMPT *verb* to try to do something

aunt—ant 1. *noun* the sister of your mother or father 2. *noun* the wife of your uncle

back•ward—BAK-werd 1. *adverb* back in the direction you came from 2. *adjective* pointing the wrong way, so the front is facing back

ba•nan•a—buh-NAN-uh *noun* a long, curved fruit with a yellow peel

bar•ber—BAHR-ber *noun* a person who cuts hair

base•ball—BAYS-bahl 1. *noun* a game played with a bat, a ball, and four bases 2. *noun* a ball used for playing baseball

base•ment—BAS-muhnt *noun* a room or rooms under a house or building

bath•room—BATH-room *noun* a room for bathing and using the toilet

beast—beest *noun* an animal or other creature that is not human and doesn't act human

beau•ti•ful—BYOO-tuh-fuhl *adjective* very pretty

bor•row—BAHR-oh *verb* when someone allows you to take something for a short time, then give it back

braid—brayd 1. *noun* hair in a rope-like style 2. *verb* to put hair in a rope-like style

bread—brehd *noun* a baked food made with flour that's used for toast and sandwiches

breathe—breeth *verb* to take in air through your mouth or nose

broth•er—BRUHTH-er *noun* a boy whose mother and father have another child

but•ter•fly—BUHT-er-fli *noun* an insect with large wings that are sometimes very colorful

cap•tain—KAP-tihn 1. *noun* the leader of a sports team 2. *noun* the leader of a ship or airplane 3. *noun* the leader of firefighters, police, or the military

car•rot—KEHR-uht *noun* a skinny orange vegetable that grows underground

cat•er•pil•lar—KAT-er-pihl-er *noun* an insect like a worm that turns into a butterfly or a moth

cheek—cheek *noun* the side of your face between your nose and your ear. You have two cheeks.

chew—choo *verb* to use your teeth to bite food in your mouth

chirp—cherp 1. *noun* the short, pretty sound a small bird makes 2. *verb* to make a chirping sound

click—klihk 1. *noun* a quick sound like teeth tapping together 2. *verb* to make a clicking sound

clos•et—CLAHZ-iht *noun* a very small room to keep clothes and shoes

co•coon—kuh-KOON *noun* a silk wrap or bag made by an insect to keep its body or eggs safe. A caterpillar goes into a cocoon while turning into a moth.

com•fort•a•ble—KUHM-fer-tuh-buhl 1. *adjective* very soft or easy, 2. *adjective* with no pain or fear

coun•try—KUHN-tree 1. *noun* the nation where you live, like the United States or Canada 2. *noun* a place far away from any city, where there is more nature

crea•ture—KREE-cher *noun* a living animal or human

croak—krohk 1. *noun* the rough, deep sound of a frog, or your voice when your throat is sore 2. *verb* to make a croaking sound

crop—krahp *noun* a planting of something, like corn, that a farmer is growing in a field

crowd—krowd *noun* a lot of people all together

def•i•ni•tion—dehf-uh-NIHSH-uhn *noun* the meaning of a word

de•scribe—dih-SKRIB *verb* to make a picture with words, like "a pretty girl in a blue dress"

dic•tion•ar•y—DIHK-shuh-nehr-ee *noun* a book filled with definitions of words

di•rec•tion—duh-REHK-shuhn 1. *noun* the way you're going, like left or north 2. *noun* an order, like "go to bed now"

el•e•va•tor—EHL-uh-vay-ter *noun* a moving box that takes you up to the high floors of a building

emp•ty—EHMP-tee *adjective* having nothing inside

en•e•my—EHN-uh-mee *noun* someone who is working against you, a foe

eve•ry•where—EHV-ree-wehr *adverb* in all places

ex•er•cise—EHK-ser-siz 1. *noun* a set of moves that work out your body 2. *noun* an activity that helps practice a lesson 3. *verb* to move your body to make it strong and fit

ex•plain—ihk-SPLAYN *verb* to tell or teach someone about something

eye•brow—I-brow *noun* the strip of hair above your eye

fail—fayl *verb* to lose, to not get what you tried for

fa•vor•ite—FA-ver-iht *adjective* the one that is liked the most

feath•er—FEHTH-er *noun* one of the soft pieces that cover a bird's body and wings

field—feeld *noun* a wide space of ground that has plants growing in it, like grass or a crop

flight—flit 1. *noun* a trip through the air, like on a plane 2. *noun* a fast getaway, escape

flock—flahk 1. *noun* a group of birds 2. *verb* to make a group, like a flock of birds

flood—fluhd 1. *noun* a lot of water that overflows from a river, or fills an area like a house 2. *verb* to fill an area with water

for•give—fer-GIHV *verb* to stop being mad and make up after a fight with someone

for•ward—FOR-werd *adverb* in a straight direction

freck•les—FREHK-lz *noun* spots on skin from the sun

fright•en—FRIT-uhn *verb* to scare somebody

frown—frown 1. *noun* a sad or mad face, the opposite of a smile 2. *verb* to make a sad or mad face

fruit—froot 1. *noun* a food that can be juicy and sweet, like an apple 2. *noun* the part of a plant that holds the seeds

gi•ant—JI-uhnt 1. *noun* a huge person or other creature out of a fairy tale 2. *adjective* very big

grand•fa•ther—GRAND-fah-*ther* 1. *noun* the father of your father or mother 2. *noun* your grandmother's husband

grand•moth•er—GRAND-muh*th*-er 1. *noun* the mother of your father or mother 2. *noun* your grandfather's wife

herd—herd 1. *noun* a group of land animals like cows 2. *verb* to make a group of animals go somewhere

hive—hiv *noun* a nest of bees, where they make honey

hus•band—HUHZ-buhnd *noun* a man who is married

in•sect—IHN-sehkt *noun* a small creature with no backbone (a bug)

is•land—I-luhnd *noun* a piece of land that is in the ocean, with water on all sides

jin•gle—JIHNG-guhl 1. *noun* the sound of a little bell, or two small pieces of metal bumping together 2. *verb* to make a jingling sound

kneel—neel *verb* to get down on your knees

lan•guage—LANG-gwihj *noun* the kind of speech used in different countries, like English or French

lar•va—LAHR-vuh *noun* a baby insect that looks like a worm. A caterpillar is the larva of a butterfly.

lawn—lawn *noun* the grass around a house

light•house—LIT-hows *noun* a tall building with a big light that helps boats see the shore

lit•ter—LIHT-er 1. *noun* trash that is on the ground 2. *verb* to leave trash on the ground

lone•ly—LOHN-lee *adjective* sad because there's nobody around

may•or—MAY-er *noun* the leader of a town or city

mean•ing—MEE-nihng *noun* the idea of a word, what it means

mod•ern—MAHD-dern *adjective* very new and up to date, not old

mon•u•ment—MAHN-yuh-muhnt *noun* anything that is put up to honor a person or event

moun•tain—MOWN-tuhn *noun* a tall peak of land, much higher than a hill

mouth—mowth 1. *noun* the hole in your face where you put your food 2. *verb* to talk with your lips without making a sound

nat•u•ral—NATCH-er-uhl 1. *adjective* the way nature made it, not changed by humans 2. *adjective* not fake

neigh•bor—NAY-ber *noun* a person who lives next door to or near you

neigh•bor•hood—NAY-ber-hud *noun* an area where people live

nois•y—NOY-zee *adjective* loud, full of sound

noun—nown *noun* a word that stands for a person, place, or thing

paint—peynt 1. *noun* color that can be put on walls or objects 2. *verb* to put color on something using paint

pred•a•tor—PREHD-uh-ter *noun* an animal or insect that hunts others for its food

reach—reech 1. *verb* to put out your hand to get something 2. *verb* to arrive at a place

re•frig•er•a•tor—rih-FRIHJ-uh-ray-ter *noun* a metal box that keeps food and drinks cold

re•spect—rih-SPEHKT 1. *noun* a feeling that you honor someone 2. *verb* to honor and show consideration for someone

rude—rood *adjective* not nice, makes other people feel bad

shade—shad *noun* a place where the sun is blocked by something, like under a tree

share—shehr 1. *noun* one person's part of something that can be split 2. *verb* to let other people use your things or eat your food 3. *verb* to use something with other people

shiv•er—SHIHV-er 1. *noun* a shake of the body 2. *verb* to shake your body, like when it's cold

side•walk—SID-wawk *noun* a smooth, hard walkway

sis•ter—SIHS-ter *noun* a girl whose mother and father have another child

skate—skayt 1. *noun* a shoe with a sharp blade that helps you slide on ice 2. *noun* a shoe with wheels that help you roll on the sidewalk 3. *verb* to use skates to move along the ground or on ice

soil—soyl 1. *noun* dirt that is used for growing plants 2. *verb* to make something dirty

speech—speech 1. *noun* words said by a person 2. *noun* a talk made in front of a crowd

spend—spehnd *verb* to use up, like money or time

spread—sprehd 1. *verb* to put something all over, like jam on bread 2. *verb* to open wide

squawk—skwahk 1. *noun* the noisy yell of a crow or other loud bird 2. *verb* to make a squawking sound

squeak—skweek 1. *noun* the high, tiny sound of a mouse, or when sneakers rub on a wood floor 2. *verb* to make a squeaking sound

squirm—skwerm *verb* to move around in a twisty-turny way

sting—stihng 1. *noun* the feeling of a bug bite or pin prick 2. *verb* to use a stinger or other sharp object to break someone's skin

stom•ach—STUHM-uhk *noun* your tummy, or belly, that tells you when you're hungry or full

stop•light—STAHP-lit *noun* a light that helps move traffic safely where two roads cross

stuffed—stuhft *adjective* filled with something, like a pillow is filled with fluff, or a belly is filled with food

suc•ceed—suhk-SEED *verb* to win, to get what you wanted

sug•gest—suhg-JEHST 1. *verb* to hint at something 2. *verb* to give an idea or plan as an option

sun•rise—SUHN-riz *noun* the time of day when the sun comes up

swal•low—SWAHL-oh *verb* to let food go from your mouth into your throat and stomach

tame—taym 1. *adjective* quiet, safe, and nice 2. *verb* to make a wild animal be nice to humans

taste—tayst 1. *noun* the way a food is salty, sweet, or icky 2. *verb* to put a bit of food in your mouth to see if you like it

teen—teen *noun* a person who is older than a child but younger than an adult

throat—throht 1. *noun* the front part of your neck 2. *noun* the tube inside your neck that goes to your stomach and your lungs

tooth•paste—TOOTH-payst *noun* a cream used to clean teeth

trav•el—TRAV-uhl 1. *noun* a visit to another place 2. *verb* to go somewhere

un•cle—UHNG-kuhl *noun* 1. the brother of your mother or father 2. *noun* the husband of your aunt

va•ca•tion—vay-KAY-shuhn 1. *noun* a break from work or school 2. *verb* to take a break, maybe travel

val•ley—VAL-ee *noun* a low spot between hills or mountains

veg•e•ta•ble—VEHJ-tuh-buhl *noun* a food that comes from a plant's leaves or roots

verb—verb *noun* a word that stands for an action, like *run*

wife—wif *noun* a woman who is married

wild—wild 1. *adjective* not tame, not safe, not able to live with humans 2. *noun* a place where people don't live, like the jungle

Answers

Page 207
1. describe
2. meaning
3. verb
4. noun
5. adjective
6. dictionary
7. definition

Page 208
1. angry
2. balloon
3. jelly
4. learn
5. machine
6. octopus
7. trouble
8. whisper

Page 209
1. verb
2. adjective
3. verb
4. noun
5. adjective
6. verb
7. noun
8. noun

Page 210
1. food
2. present
3. traffic
4. rock
5. bagpipes
6. monarch
7. unique
8. hawk

Page 211
1. 3
2. 4
3. 2
4. 4
5. 2
6. 1
7. 3
8. 1

Page 213
1. giant
2. fail
3. succeed
4. predator
5. arrive
6. beautiful
7. attempt
8. enemy

Page 214
1. opposite
2. same
3. opposite
4. opposite
5. same
6. same
7. opposite
8. same

Page 215
1. Kira
2. Joe
3. Larry
4. Darla
5. Talia

Page 216
ACROSS
2. arrive
4. giant
5. fail

DOWN
1. beautiful
3. enemy

Page 217
1. 3
2. NO
3. **Suggestion:** I don't skate very well.

Page 219
1. everywhere
2. sunrise
3. baseball
4. sidewalk
5. lighthouse
6. toothpaste
7. bathroom
8. stoplight

Page 220
1. sunrise
2. baseball
3. toothpaste
4. bathroom
5. sidewalk
6. stoplight

Page 221
1. grand + father = grandfather
2. skate + board = skateboard
3. play + ground = playground
4. news + paper = newspaper
5. green + house = greenhouse

Page 222
sunrise → sunset
troublemaker → peacemaker
somebody → nobody
downstairs → upstairs
nighttime → daytime
everything → nothing
bedtime → playtime
highway → sidewalk

Page 223
1. starfish, football, ~~adjective,~~ ~~predator~~
2. ~~enemy,~~ playground, everybody, ~~arrive~~
3. lighthouse, ~~beautiful,~~ ~~dictionary,~~ blueberry
4. stoplight, ~~unhappy,~~ nothing, ~~syllable~~

Page 225
1. frown
2. throat
3. mouth
4. braid
5. freckles
6. eyebrow
7. stomach
8. cheek

Page 226
ACROSS
3. throat
5. cheek

DOWN
1. frown
2. stomach
4. freckles

Page 227
1. finger, throat, ~~verb,~~ ~~definition~~
2. ~~sunrise, fail,~~ freckles, mouth
3. arm, ~~sidewalk,~~ stomach, ~~attempt~~
4. ~~syllable,~~ eyebrow, ~~giant,~~ cheek

Page 228
1. Tyara
2. Connor
3. Carly
4. Jordan
5. Doug

Page 229
1. cheek
2. mouth
3. stomach
4. eyebrow
5. freckles
6. throat

Page 231
1. squirm
2. kneel
3. shiver
4. chew
5. swallow
6. reach
7. breathe
8. exercise

Page 232
1. Maddy is chewing gum.
2. Mr. Santos is exercising.
3. Ty kneels on the ground.
4. The baby reaches for her bottle.

Page 233
1. shiver
2. exercise
3. reach
4. squirming
5. swallow
6. kneel
7. chew
8. breathe

Page 234
1. squirm
2. breathe
3. beautiful
4. reach
5. shiver
6. swallow
7. chew
8. enemy

Page 235

Page 237
1. teen
2. adult
3. crowd
4. actor
5. barber
6. mayor
7. captain
8. neighbor

Page 238
1. crowd
2. mayor
3. captain
4. actor
5. barber
6. neighbor

Page 239
ACROSS
2. teen
4. adult
5. barber

DOWN
1. neighbor
3. mayor

Page 240
1. Leena
2. Serena
3. Hunter
4. Cyrus
5. Bart

Page 241

Page 243
1. respect
2. share
3. borrow
4. explain
5. suggest
6. agree
7. frighten
8. forgive

Answers

Page 244
1. Tom does not respect Donna.
2. Jean shares her pizza with Mike.
3. Sondra frightens Neal.
4. Neal forgives Sondra.

Page 245
1. borrow
2. explain
3. respect
4. beautiful
5. share
6. neighbor
7. enemy
8. agree

Page 246
1. explain
2. forgive
3. respect
4. suggests
5. agree
6. shares
7. frighten
8. borrow

Page 247
1. ~~enemy~~, ~~beautiful~~, forgive, attempt
2. frighten, ~~scary~~, exercise, d~~efinition~~
3. ~~verb~~, share, ~~throat~~, borrow
4. respect, ~~sidewalk~~, suggest, ~~idea~~

Page 249
1. husband
2. grandfather
3. sister
4. uncle
5. wife
6. brother
7. aunt
8. grandmother

Page 250
ACROSS   DOWN
2. grandfather   1. brother
3. husband

parent: a mother or father
sibling: a brother or sister
spouse: a husband or wife

Page 251
1. grandmother
2. grandfather
3. wife
4. husband
5. aunt
6. uncle
7. brother
8. sister

Page 252
1. Jen is Peter's sister.
2. Stan is Sheila's husband.
3. Greg is Karl's grandfather.
4. This is my aunt.

Page 253
1. grandfather, daughter, ~~frighten~~, ~~frown~~
2. son, ~~bathroom~~, ~~suggest~~, sister
3. ~~predator~~, ~~agree~~, mother, aunt
4. ~~respect~~, uncle, brother, ~~elephant~~

Page 255
1. empty
2. closet
3. basement
4. favorite
5. refrigerator
6. paint
7. comfortable
8. lawn

Page 256
1. refrigerator
2. empty
3. favorite
4. comfortable
5. lawn

Page 257
ACROSS   DOWN
3. closet   1. paint
4. empty   2. basement
5. lawn

Page 258
1. The box is empty.
2. The lawn is green.
3. That chair looks comfortable.
4. That's Dipti's favorite doll.

Page 259

Page 261
1. taste
2. carrot
3. banana
4. vegetable
5. stuffed
6. fruit
7. spread
8. bread

Page 262
1. Crispin
2. Lyle
3. Shama
4. Mai
5. Val

Page 263
1. vegetable
2. vegetable
3. fruit
4. fruit
5. vegetable
6. vegetable
7. fruit
8. vegetable

Page 264
1. carrots
2. taste
3. spread
4. bread
5. fruit
6. stuffed
7. banana
8. vegetables

Page 265

Page 267
1. flock
2. wild
3. beast
4. flight
5. creature
6. tame
7. feather
8. herd

Page 268
1. beasts
2. tame
3. wild
4. flocks
5. feathers
6. herds

Page 269
ACROSS   DOWN
1. flock   2. creature
3. herd   4. feather
4. flight

Page 270
1. A flock of geese flew by.
2. Mr. Tibbles is tame.
3. This bird has green feathers.
4. We are in the wild.

Page 271

Page 273
1. cocoon
2. insect
3. antennae
4. caterpillar
5. sting
6. butterfly
7. larva
8. hive

Page 274
1. Tinky
2. Slinky
3. Binky
4. Dinky
5. Pinky

Page 275
1. sting
2. antennae
3. butterflies
4. larva
5. hives
6. cocoon
7. caterpillars
8. insects

Page 276
ACROSS   DOWN
2. insect   1. sting
5. antennae   3. cocoon
6. hive   4. larva

Page 277

Page 279
1. noisy
2. chirp
3. squeak
4. click
5. jingle
6. speech
7. squawk
8. croak

Answers

Page 280

ACROSS	DOWN
3. click	1. squawk
5. noisy	2. jingle
6. squeak	4. croak

Page 281
1. croak
2. noisy
3. squeaking
4. speech
5. clicking
6. jingle
7. squawks
8. chirping

Page 282
1. roar
2. squeak
3. honk
4. crunch
5. squawk
6. click
7. chirp
8. croak

Page 283
1. click, ~~carrot, larva,~~ hoot
2. ~~paint, teen,~~ roar, squawk
3. honk, chirp, ~~taste, kneel~~
4. squeak, ~~cheek,~~ screech, ~~frown~~

Page 285
1. mountain
2. shade
3. crop
4. valley
5. field
6. natural
7. flood
8. soil

Page 286
1. natural
2. field
3. shade
4. valley
5. soiled
6. crops
7. mountain
8. flooded

Page 287
1. Vernon is sitting in the shade.
2. Corn is growing in this field.
3. This soil is good for growing things.
4. The house is in the valley.

Page 288
1. opposite
2. opposite
3. same
4. same
5. same
6. opposite
7. opposite
8. opposite

Page 289

Page 291
1. neighborhood
2. litter
3. modern
4. elevator
5. spend
6. lonely
7. monument
8. rude

Page 292
1. lonely
2. neighborhood
3. spend
4. monument
5. rude
6. modern
7. elevator

Page 293

ACROSS	DOWN
1. modern	1. monument
2. lonely	2. litter
3. elevator	

Page 295
1. country
2. island
3. backward
4. travel
5. direction
6. vacation
7. forward
8. language

Page 296
1. Fiona
2. Chantal
3. Jorge
4. Mona
5. Simon

Page 297
1. forward
2. vacation
3. country
4. traveled
5. backward
6. islands
7. directions
8. language

Page 298
1. Staci is walking forward.
2. Martin is on a mountain.
3. Xyqx speaks a different language.
4. Joel is in the country.

Page 299

Page 300
1. crowd
2. basement
3. stuffed
4. tame
5. agree
6. predator
7. rude
8. noise

Page 301
1. country
2. adjectives
3. definition
4. dictionary
5. verb
6. opposite
7. compound
8. language

Page 302
1. verb
2. noun
3. verb
4. adjective
5. verb
6. verb
7. noun

Page 303
1. ~~comfortable,~~ monument, ~~forgive,~~ toothpaste
2. flight, ~~lonely,~~ stomach, ~~borrow~~
3. ~~succeed,~~ wife, basement, ~~empty~~
4. ~~arrive,~~ elevator, ~~rude,~~ neighborhood